LEGAL
COUNSEL

06/04

NATIONAL LIBRARY OF CANADA CATALOGUING IN PUBLICATION DATA

Vandor, Les
Legal counsel: frequently asked questions about the law

Contents: bk. 1. An introduction to the legal system, individual rights and employment rights bk. 2. Property rights, family and divorce and company rights bk. 3.
Retirement, representation and wills.

ISBN 1-55022-483-2 V.1.   ISBN 1-55022-485-9 V.2.   ISBN 1-55022-486-7 V.3.

1. Law Canada – Popular works. 1. Title.

KE447.V35 2001   349.71   C2001-900823-7

Author photo on back cover by Marilyn Mikkelsen
Cover and text design by Tania Craan
Layout by Wiesia Kolasinska

Printed by AGMV

Distributed in Canada by
General Distribution Services,
325 Humber College Blvd.,
Toronto, ON M9W 7C3

Published by ECW PRESS
2120 Queen Street East, Suite 200
Toronto, ON M4E 1E2
ecwpress.com

This book is set in Bembo and Futura.

PRINTED AND BOUND IN CANADA

The publication of *Legal Counsel* has been generously supported by the
Government of Canada through the Book Publishing
Industry Development Program. Canadä

Disclaimer: The questions and answers that follow are meant as a guide.
You are encouraged to consult with your own legal practitioner for
details as to your particular situation.

LEGAL
COUNSEL

FREQUENTLY ASKED
QUESTIONS
ABOUT THE LAW

BOOK ONE

An Introduction to the Legal System,
Individual Rights, and Employment Rights

LES VANDOR, QC

ECW PRESS

To Tibor Joseph Vandor,
my father

TABLE OF CONTENTS

DEBTS: credit cards, bankruptcy

BANKING: enforcing a letter of credit, security for costs

RRSPs AND PENSIONS: RRSPs, RRIFs, and RESPs, collecting pensions, tax shelters, tax loopholes, mutual funds

COPYRIGHT: photograph ownership, copyright of business names, expiry of copyright, patents, TV images

Y2K: liability for failure of computers, insurance coverage

CHAPTER THREE — EMPLOYMENT RIGHTS

INTRODUCTION

CAUSE: compensation, changing terms of employment (employee's rights), termination of employment and wrongful dismissal

MONEY: severance packages

NONCOMPETITION: use of company information upon termination of employment, prevention of employees from working for another organization, employee rights when contract not fulfilled

DOWNSIZING: actuarially reduced pensions, severance packages on privatization, year-to-year contracts, rules to follow when dismissing employees

RETIREMENT: mandatory at age 65, challenges

CHANGES AT WORK: increase in employment hours, changes from long-term to contractual employment

MATERNITY: discrimination in selection for job promotion, single parents

DISCLOSURE: psychological disability, employer obligations in seasonal work

STUDENTS: inadequate payment for work performed

INJURIES: work-related injuries

SMALL BUSINESSES: co-ownership, injuries and Worker's Compensation

UNIONS: putting forth individual complaints to the union

WORK PRODUCT: ownership of products designed for a company

EXTRA WORK: training for higher-paying jobs

WORK ENVIRONMENT: smoking at work and health-related obligations

QUALIFICATIONS: misstatement in letters of reference, sharing of personal information, sample letters of reference

Foreword

by the former Chief Justice of British Columbia

I was pleased when my longtime friend Les Vandor, QC, asked me to write a foreword to the Legal Counsel series of books he has written answering the most often asked questions about the law. This is a project that needs a lot of attention, and I applaud every attempt to explain and clarify the law.

It is often said, incorrectly I believe, that the law is a mystery to most people. That is because everything we do not understand is a mystery to us. The law can be very straightforward, as in the formation of a contract or the definition of negligence, or exceedingly difficult, as in the defence of insanity in a criminal law context or the interpretation of some sections of the Income Tax Act. What makes the difference, of course, is information.

Thus, the most junior lawyer knows that a contract is formed when an offer is accepted; that negligence is doing what a reasonable person would not do or not doing what a reasonable person would do; that the defence of insanity is more difficult and that even lawyers need to look at the most recent decision of the Supreme Court of Canada, *R. v. Stone*, to understand this particular defence; and, as some lawyers say, that only God knows what some sections of the Income Tax Act mean.

So those who wonder about a legal question are searching for information that will help them to answer their questions or to understand that the complexities of some laws — usually dictated by the complexities of society — require much study and research before some questions can be answered.

What is often not understood is that when persons disagree about any matter, legal or otherwise, they are probably operating from different databases. I often think that, if only the public knew what I know about a case, it would agree with my decisions much more readily than is sometimes the case and vice versa in some cases. So it is important for the judiciary and the legal profession to provide information to the public so that it can more readily understand why the law is the way it is and why cases are decided the way they are.

Great strides have been made recently in this direction. Most courts now publish all their decisions on the Internet. Some authors are writing books about the law in engaging and understandable terms. I have tried to explain the judiciary and the criminal law in a legal compendium I have published on the Internet, and Les Vandor has tried to make the law more understandable through the medium of his radio show.

He has now gone one step further in agreeing to write three books about the law. I am happy to have this opportunity to congratulate him for his energy and industry. I am confident that his endeavours will add greatly to public understanding of the law.

The Hon. Allan McEachern
former Chief Justice of British Columbia

Foreword

by the former Chief Justice of Nova Scotia

This book deals with many of the problems that confront and confound all of us in our daily lives whether it be on a personal, family or business level.

Owning a home is the goal of most Canadian families. Acquiring a house appears to be a relatively simple proposition. But houses sit on land, and therein arise some of the most complex problems people face, especially if adequate investigation and care have not been taken before the contract to purchase is signed. Those who buy or rent a condominium or duplex or apartment often wish, after the event, they were forewarned of pending pitfalls.

Consider the family cottage. Parents, convinced that there will never be dissension among their children, who "love the cottage," would be shocked after their demise to find that war has broken out among their offspring. On occasion, ownership and control of the beloved cottage become so fractured that it ends up being sold for the nonpayment of property taxes.

Unfortunately, many families are confronted with differences that lead to separation and divorce. Such circumstances are fraught with myriad difficult issues over who will own property and how the custody of children will be settled. It is much easier for judges to decide who should get Aunt Jessie's vase than how the children will be supported and by whom they will be raised.

None of us needs to establish a large company with its shares traded on a stock exchange to become involved in a corporate or commercial venture that can make us rich or do us in. Often a good idea is worth being patented or developed into a small business. Working with a friend or colleague may lead to the suggestion that a partnership be formed. The implications that result from totally innocent business associations can be devastating if plans are not properly documented.

The one thing that makes this book so useful is that in it Les Vandor, QC, has collected the real life experiences of Canadians. While it is not designed to be a legal text, it offers a practical guide to problems and their solutions.

For all of this, we owe Les Vandor our thanks.

The Hon. Lorne Clarke, OC, QC,
former Chief Justice of Nova Scotia

Preface

People write books for many reasons. Some write for money, while others have stories to tell. Some write to fill personal or social needs. I wrote as a result of a number of factors that seemed to coalesce at one time.

The first factor was a client who didn't pay me. I thought at the time that the advice I had given was good. Since I had done the research for the opinion, why not put the information I had gleaned from various sources to good use? I approached the CBC and suggested a call-in show on the topic I had researched. That was in 1992. Thus began for me a stint on radio giving free legal advice. I must thank the CBC (and in particular Dave Stephens and Elizabeth Hay) and its many listeners, whose questions are in this book.

The second factor was a neighbour who lived up the street. We have a variety of people who live nearby. We have economists, physicians, businesspeople, consultants, and military personnel. We have street parties. At a recent party, a neighbour in the book-publishing business suggested I write a book. I said maybe since he was the host and I was a polite guest. Were we under the influence of good cheer, or was this a serious option? I'd get back to him.

The third factor was a propensity to write. I scribbled on various pieces of paper and was fortunate to have had two pieces published in the *Globe and Mail*. I had always dreamed of writing a book of short stories. Law was not on the list. Yet law afforded me the opportunity to write.

In the weeks that followed, I was preoccupied with my ailing father. In the hospital, I engaged in small talk. I suggested a book, and my father said yes. I went home and began to write.

My aim in writing was to increase the public's basic understanding of the law. I didn't need to write just to see my name in print. My clients gave me that in some of the high-profile cases I had the honour of handling. These cases ranged from suing a TV station (the media loved that one) to fighting Revenue Canada (the public loved that one). I hope I have met the goal of public education.

I would like to thank my father and Robert Ferguson (my neighbour). My wife and children took this project in stride, what with all the other crazy things I do. I thank my assistant, Robyn-Erin, for retyping various drafts and reminding me of some of the clients who walked in off the street. Without them, there would be no book. Let me also thank Dallas Harrison, my editor, who fixed my sentence structure. I wish that I could use his talents in my legal drafting. Thank you to all.

Introduction

The law is not a big, scary, incomprehensible beast. Dick the Butcher (an associate of Jack Cade), not Shakespeare, would have killed all lawyers, but lawyers and the law are part of our society, where rules and regulations govern our daily lives.

In primitive societies, the leader of a group or tribal chief would make decisions on a daily basis to settle disputes and set priorities. As a society evolved, the lord of the manor, and ultimately the king or queen, would establish rules and regulations for the orderly conduct of daily affairs. When problems arose, he or she would render a decision. Often the aggrieved persons would be so emotionally caught up with the problem that they would have a friend or family member assist them in advancing their cases. Thus began the idea of advocacy and ultimately a separate profession of lawyers.

While there may be good and bad lawyers, just like there are good and bad plumbers, a lawyer can assist not only in advocating your interests but also in protecting your rights. A classic example is your last will, in which you determine how to distribute your worldly goods after death. A lawyer can assist you in drafting the appropriate document.

Criticisms of lawyers often centre on the use of archaic terms. The use of legal terms is slowly giving way to plain language, as evidenced by insurance contracts that have become more and more readable. This is a direct result of the public's demand for straightforward language.

The more the public demands this simple language, the more the legal profession will adopt it, if only for self-preservation.

In Canada, the system of justice is administered by federally and provincially appointed judges in every province and territory. It is no longer the case that the king or queen alone can dispense justice, given the size and complexity of our society. There are over 1,000 federally appointed judges who have the mandate of interpreting the laws passed by Parliament. They also settle individual disputes as they come before the courts.

Most provinces and territories have an entry-level court, often called a superior court. The superior court handles most disputes. If the parties are not satisfied with the result, there are provincial appeal courts that review and, if necessary, reverse the lower court's decision. The ultimate appeal court is the Supreme Court of Canada, which hears appeals from the provinces in both civil and criminal matters.

Judges are often criticized for making erroneous decisions or creating new laws, a domain traditionally reserved for Parliament. It is often suggested that those decisions are direct results of the input made by clients and their lawyers. If a client fails to tell a lawyer the full story, then the results can often be skewed. Similarly, if a lawyer fails to fully advance all relevant legal arguments, then a court cannot be blamed for rendering a decision that may not cover all issues. As a result, it is vital that individuals fully disclose their problems to their solicitors. To encourage full disclosure, the concept of solicitor–client privilege, similar to the privilege between a priest and a penitent, has been developed. The information given to a lawyer remains confidential and fully protected by law. In this fashion, a lawyer can be armed with all the relevant facts and protect or advance a client's interests to the fullest.

The fear often expressed by clients is that, if they tell the full story, a lawyer may refuse to take the case. A lawyer, and ultimately a court, must be armed with all the facts to properly solve a legal problem. Full disclosure is essential to this process and must be encouraged.

Criticism has been levied against lawyers for taking too much time explaining the law in a particular case. What I hope to do with this book is offer basic information on various areas of the law and provide answers to the most frequently asked questions. I hope that the book will assist readers in demystifying the law and understanding its basic concepts.

The questions that follow have been frequently asked by clients and CBC Radio listeners. Each section explains a legal concept, followed by the basic questions and answers in each area. You will also see inserts that provide further explanations, legal trivia, or stories to illustrate points. I also hope to debunk a few legal myths.

There are three books in the series. What I hope to do in book one is explain the legal system and individual rights. In book two, I will cover issues surrounding the family and buying a home. Finally, in book three, I will cover retirement and estate planning. In this way, I will cover an individual's life, at least from a legal point of view, from birth to death.

Remember, every case is different, and every new fact puts a wrinkle in the case. Provincial laws vary and often change. This book should be used as a guide and not necessarily the definitive solution to each situation. Yet basic principles can be explained and are applicable in many day-to-day situations.

CHAPTER ONE

Introduction to the Legal System

The Canadian legal system has many players. We will start with you and me as basic citizens whose rights may have been infringed by a neighbour, a professional, a school board, or a local governmental authority.

If you feel strongly enough about your rights, you can complain to your member of Parliament, or you can sue. That is where the court system kicks in. You can sue on your own, or you can hire a lawyer. Either way there are forms to be filed and clerks ready to receive your written complaint. That is the beginning of a lawsuit.

A lawyer, or even your neighbour if you have sued him or her over a fence or over noise problems and he or she has decided to act without a lawyer, will respond to the complaint, called a **claim**. After the lawsuit has started, there will be an exchange of documents, if any, in support of your claim. Ultimately, the matter will proceed to court unless there is a settlement, and a judge will hear your complaint. Your neighbour, using that example, will respond with his or her version of events. Thereafter, the judge will make a ruling.

If either party is unhappy, an appeal to a higher court can be made. A hearing will be held, and once again a ruling will be made. If after that you are still unhappy, you can appeal to the **Supreme Court of Canada**. Be warned, however, that it will only hear matters that touch on all Canadians with similar concerns.

This simple summary focuses on the fact that, if you have a right that has been infringed, you can enforce that right through the proper channels. You are, as they say, not alone. Throughout this process, court officials will assist you in completing the required forms.

After having decided to sue, where do you go? Most provinces and territories have an entry-level court called a **small claims court**, and generally these courts hear disputes with a value of up to $10,000. In some cases, it is not cost effective to hire a lawyer and spend, say, $3,000 in legal fees in order to recover $5,000 from the claim. The small claims court is meant to be a quick and efficient way to enforce your rights.

For claims in excess of $10,000, the entry-level court is called a **superior court**. The forms and rules of this court are more technical and specialized, and often you will need a lawyer to help you navigate through the process. For example, in a superior court lawsuit, you or your lawyer can question one witness from the opposing side to get at all the facts and relevant documents. This is called a **discovery**. The proceedings are recorded, and the transcript is available at trial. It is often used to "trip up" the witness if his or her story changes at trial.

Should you choose to go to the small claims court, clerks will assist you in preparing the initial documents, setting out what you want, from whom, and why. They will assist you in having the claim properly stamped by a court official and properly sent to the person you are suing. When it comes to a trial, small claims court judges will explain what you have to prove in a court of law and which documents should be put before the court in support of your claim. Similarly, when it comes to higher-level courts, clerks will assist you in filing the appropriate forms.

Figure 1: Basic Levels of Courts

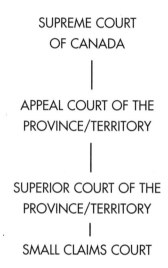

SUPREME COURT
OF CANADA

APPEAL COURT OF THE
PROVINCE/TERRITORY

SUPERIOR COURT OF THE
PROVINCE/TERRITORY

SMALL CLAIMS COURT

Throughout the process, it's you the complainant or, if you have a lawyer, you the client who drives the justice system. If you are unhappy, you can complain. If you sue, you set the terms, for it is *you* the client who ultimately calls the shots.

A word about what follows. Over the 20 years I have answered questions from clients, and in the past 10 years from CBC Radio listeners, there have been recurrent themes. Can I sue a doctor? How do I present my case? Why are there delays in the court system? Is mediation an alternative? Can I complain about my lawyer or the judge? Can I sue a broker? Can I fight a traffic ticket? I have grouped these types of questions into four broad categories: lawsuits, mediation, lawyers and judges, and suing other entities. What follows are the most frequently asked questions and their answers in each category.

Some say that the legal system cannot be explained in simple terms; after all, lawyers can spend more than four years learning the ins and outs of the law and the courts. However, there are some basic principles that can be easily explained.

Many of us have seen or heard of the movie *The Paper Chase*. In one of its opening sequences, a law professor explains that he will shape the students' minds and change their ways of thinking. Eventually, he will make them into lawyers. Although legal training involves shaping people's minds, after several years of practice most lawyers will tell you that common sense prevails. In other words, many problems can be solved by applying simple logic rather than the strict provisions of one law or another. While brain surgery cannot be explained in simple terms, some legal concepts can be set out in the questions and answers that follow.

This text does not have the definitive answer to every question, since laws vary across provinces and territories. Four years of learning cannot be summarized in one book. Yet what follows is applicable in many day-to-day situations.

Lawsuits

Q: What are the normal courses of the lawsuit?

A: A legal document called a **statement of claim** is prepared. It sets out why you (the **plaintiff**) are suing the other person and for what amount of money. The person sued (the **defendant**) then files what is called a **statement of defence**, which sets out why he or she is not responsible. Thereafter, each side is questioned under oath (**discovery**) in a private session in the presence of your lawyer and the opposing lawyer. Finally, there is a trial (unless the matter has settled) either before a judge alone or before a judge and jury. You and your lawyer will then set out to prove that your case has merit with oral testimony and written documents in support of your claim.

Figure 2: Timeline for a Lawsuit

STATEMENT OF CLAIM	STATEMENT OF DEFENCE	QUESTIONING UNDER OATH	TRIAL

Q: How do I present a case in court?

A: Once in court, the plaintiff, the person suing, goes first. He or she outlines the story from beginning to end. If other people are required to add to the picture, they tell their stories. In this way, the judge gets the full picture. The defendant, the party being sued, goes next and presents his or her case in the same fashion, with witnesses adding to the story as necessary. This is called **testifying at trial**. When all the people have testified, each side is given the opportunity to summarize the case and convince the judge why he or she should win. The judge then considers the evidence and the summaries and renders a decision. That decision may be made immediately or after a few days of consideration.

Q: Is it more difficult to sue a specialist physician versus a general practitioner?

A: Yes. Specialists are judged by stricter standards, and you will be required to produce a report from another specialist who disagrees with the original method of treatment.

Q: Can a dentist be sued?

A: Yes. Any professional who fails to live up to an industry-set professional standard can be held responsible in a court of law. If you sue, you will need an independent report by a recognized expert setting out the standard and detailing how the professional failed to meet that standard.

When you feel wronged by some person or corporation, you should write a letter setting out your concerns. If no reply is received or if the reply in unsatisfactory, go one level up, say to a head office or boss. If after all this you are still unhappy, have a lawyer write a letter. Only as a last recourse should you consider suing, since it is time consuming and expensive.

Q: Can I sue an insurance company?

A: Lawsuits should not be started for frivolous claims; however, if an insurance company has failed to provide agreed-upon coverage, like any other entity it can be sued.

Q: Can I sue another driver in a motor vehicle accident?

A: Depending on where you live, the right to sue as a result of a motor vehicle accident may be restricted. The prudent course is always to contact your insurance company and ask it which rights are available to sue or obtain compensation.

Q: There was alleged fraud in a mortgage transaction. It was alleged that the broker conspired with a financial institution. Who should be sued?

A: If the fraud can be proven by documentary or other evidence, the prudent course is to sue all the parties until enough evidence is produced by any of the parties being sued that it was not involved. In that case, the party not involved would be released from the lawsuit, and the party responsible would be taken to court.

Once your case has been argued and you have a judgment, the court system is there to help you collect your winnings should the defendant in a lawsuit fail to pay. The system allows you to seize assets (via a **bailiff** or **sheriff** — these are court officials), and until you are paid, interest accumulates on your money judgment.

Q: Can I collect interest on an outstanding judgment?

A: When a judgment is granted, it automatically collects interest at a rate set by the province or territory.

Q: How do I enforce a small claims court judgment?

A: Once a judgment is obtained, a bailiff steps in after the appropriate forms have been filed. The bailiff can seize bank accounts or other assets in order to collect money owed to you.

Q: A person was sued in one province and now lives in another. Can his or her property be seized?

A: There are provisions in law that recognize judgments from province to province. If the judgment is registered in the province where the assets are located, it can be enforced by a bailiff, who can seize and sell assets.

If you are unhappy with the result of a trial, you can either forget the matter or appeal the decision. The rules of court require that an appeal be launched fairly quickly. In some cases, you have only seven days to appeal.

An appeal can be expensive since it involves your lawyer's time and will often be set back by two years because of court delays. (Some courts have successfully reduced those delays.) Most appeals are heard by a panel of three judges who will consider all the evidence and law. They will then render a decision in your case.

If you are still unhappy, you can appeal to the Supreme Court of Canada. That court, however, restricts the types of cases it hears. Generally, it hears matters of national importance. For example, your lawsuit over car repairs will not make it to that court unless the issue of repairs affects all other car owners in Canada.

Q: Why do courts limit the time that appeals can be argued?

A: The trial is the place to put in all the evidence and argue the applicable law. Appeals are often based on narrow points, and appeal courts do not retry the whole case. Appeals are therefore limited in terms of what is reviewed and how long a matter is heard.

Limitation Periods for Lawsuits in Ontario

The law requires individuals to enforce their rights within a set period of time. This provides certainty in day-to-day activities so that, 20 or 30 years from now, you do not have to worry about what you did today that may have caused injury to someone else.

So, for example, if an architect has misdesigned a renovation, you have six years to sue. If you have been assaulted by someone, you have four years to sue. If you want to complain about air travel, you have two years to sue.

In some cases, the time frames, called **limitation periods**, are quite short. In construction matters, you have 45 days to "preserve" your lien — that is, register the claim. The time runs from the date that the work ended or was completed. If you are defamed in a newspaper or radio broadcast, you must give notice within six weeks after the defamation has come to your attention. If you are injured on a municipal roadway, you have seven days for an urban municipality and 10 days for a county or township to give notice of your injuries, and you have three months from the time the damages occurred to sue. You have two years to sue as a result of a highway traffic accident, and you have six months to sue a hospital after the act or omission was committed.

If there is no specific law governing the person you wish to sue, the general rule is six years from the time the incident occurred. Courts may use a small amount of discretion to extend the time period in which you can sue.

Q: Twenty years ago, an alleged sexual assault took place while the individual was in a neighbour's home. Is it too late to bring legal proceedings?

A: Recent cases have demonstrated that it is never too late to raise issues like assault. It very much depends on an individual's will to proceed, given that he or she will have to relive the incident, which may be buried in the past. The first step is to approach the police and file a complaint. If the police refuse to prosecute, any individual can press charges by appearing before a justice of the peace at the local court house and setting out the nature and details of the complaint.

Q: How do I charge someone with assault?

A: There are two ways. The first is to contact the local police authorities and explain the situation. If they believe there is enough evidence, they will charge a person with assault. If they are not convinced there is enough evidence, any individual can press charges against any other person by convincing a justice of the peace that the incident in question took place.

Q: A lawsuit has gone on for eight years. Why is it taking so long?

A: In complex matters, whether they are criminal or civil in nature, all the necessary facts must be brought forward. This may take some time. If, on the other hand, lawyers have been dragging their feet, it may be time to obtain a second opinion to see why the matter has taken so long.

Q: Seventeen months after a trial, additional evidence was uncovered. What options are available?

A: If the evidence was unavailable at the time of the trial and would dramatically change the result, the parties should return to court to see if the judgment should be cancelled in light of the new evidence.

The Supreme Court of Canada

The Supreme Court is the ultimate appeal court in Canada. It hears appeals from all provinces and territories.

Quebec has a **civil code** dating back to Emperor Napoleon of France. This code sets out legal principles, and Quebec judges interpret the written word based on the facts of the case being tried. The rest of Canada has a system of laws based on British law, called **the common law**. It is based on unwritten principles that are often repeated in judgments. These judgments have the force of law. As both systems of law evolved, more and more laws were written down under the British system, and more and more latitude was given to Napoleonic judges.

Since the Supreme Court hears appeal cases from Quebec, its rulings carry the force of law in that province and beyond. Because Quebec has a comprehensive code, other provinces have begun setting more and more laws down on paper in the form of legislation or codes (e.g., the Labour Code). Hence, the two systems of law in Canada are slowly melding.

Legal Fees

Lawsuits can be expensive. Court fees have to be paid when you start a lawsuit, and your lawyer has to be paid.

Lawyers charge by the hour, and after a day in court you may face a bill for $3,000 to $5,000. If you win, part of your costs may be paid by the losing side in what is called an **order for costs**. You can win the lawsuit for, say, $10,000, and you can get your legal costs paid. If you lose, you pay your lawyer, and you may be ordered by the court to pay the winner's lawyer. It can therefore be costly if you lose.

An alternative way to pay your lawyer is to apply for and be granted **legal aid**. Legal aid is a provincial system of paying for legal costs if you meet your province's means test on income. For example, in some provinces you have to earn less than $23,000 a year in order to qualify for legal aid.

If you are part of a group that has been wronged, you can start a **class action suit** on behalf of all the people with the same problem. In some provinces, funds are available to pay for the class action, and members of the class may contribute toward your legal claim fund.

You will have to weigh the costs of a lawsuit versus the rights in question.

Q: How do I apply for legal aid?

A: You apply to a provincial government agency (the Legal Aid Office), asking it to pay for your lawyer's time and expenses. You have to qualify depending on your income, and the amount varies from province to province. Once the Legal Aid Office determines that you are entitled to have your legal fees paid, it issues a certificate that is then taken to the lawyer, who then sends his or her bill to the legal aid system directly for the expenses incurred on your behalf.

Q: What are the costs of starting a class action suit, and who is responsible for the costs of the suit when it is completed?

A: Other than the lawyer's time, the only other cost involved in starting a class action or any other lawsuit is the filing fee required to have the court's stamp placed on the lawsuit. The stamp certifies that a lawsuit has been started. For class action suits, special provisions in the law may provide provincial government funds to pay for the costs associated with the lawsuit. Generally, if you lose a lawsuit, you are responsible for paying your own costs, and you may be required to contribute toward the costs incurred by the winning side.

Weird and Wonderful Laws

We've all heard that *ignorance* of the law is no excuse. It's actually part of the Criminal Code.

You can prevent a *trespasser* from taking your property as long as you don't strike or cause bodily harm to the trespasser.

You can't alarm the *queen*.

As a parent, you may have been tempted at times to read the *Riot Act* to your kids. It's actually part of our law, and when invoked the police or other deputized individuals must use these magic words: "Her Majesty the Queen charges and commands all persons being assembled immediately to disperse and peaceably to depart to their habitations or their lawful business on pain of being guilty of an offence for which, on conviction, they may be sentenced to imprisonment for life. GOD SAVE THE QUEEN."

As you would suspect, *duelling* in any form is illegal.

It's illegal to stop the *clergy* on their way home from a service, a law no doubt meant to protect them from unpopular sermons.

It's illegal to spread false *news*. Is that not an oxymoron?

Do you flip a coin to see who buys the coffee at the office? It's illegal to *bet* without a licence.

It's illegal to disturb another person's *oysters*.

Harry Potter fans beware. It's illegal to pretend to use *witchcraft*.

It's illegal to sell defective *stores* (goods) to the government.

As a kid, did you ever place a *penny* on a railway tracks and keep the squashed coin as a keepsake? It's illegal to deface currency.

In the early 1990s, it was illegal to wear spandex *shorts* in Saskatchewan. In the 1950s, it was illegal for women in Quebec to wear any type of shorts in public.

If you travel with a cart on a highway, your horse or other animal must have at least two *bells* attached to the harness. If not, you face a five-dollar fine.

The Jury System

Juries hear the evidence in a particular case, withdraw to a separate room to consider the evidence, and, as we have all seen on TV, render a verdict. What happens inside a jury room is protected by law and remains confidential. This has been a fundamental pillar in the way juries work. Section 649 of the Criminal Code of Canada makes it a criminal offence for a juror to disclose any information relating to the proceedings of the jury. This rule goes back to the eighteenth century.

Recently, however, the Ontario Court of Appeal and the Supreme Court of Canada questioned whether this principle should remain. The case in question involved a bid to reopen a murder conviction, with one of the key pieces of evidence being the testimony of a juror as to what had happened behind closed doors. Although ultimately the juror did not testify, the door was left open for future cases in which it could be shown that failure to disclose what happened in the jury room may deprive a person of a fair trial contrary to the principles of fundamental justice.

Q: How does a jury system work?

A: Juries are generally available in civil or criminal matters. They are called the **triers of fact** — that is, they determine who is to be believed when there are two versions of an event. Juries are selected from voters' lists, which contain only the names, addresses, and occupations of individuals. No other information is available, so often jurors are selected by lawyers based on the type of case. If, for example, an employee is suing a boss, lawyers will shy away from managers or executives as jury members since they may tend to make decisions based on their personal experiences. There is limited questioning of potential jurors and in some cases only if a judge allows. Once chosen, the jury will listen to the evidence and be asked to render a decision based on the evidence heard and the questions put to them. Both the lawyers and the judge presiding over the case will explain what jurors are to do and how they are to reach a decision or verdict.

In the United States, unlike in Canada, you are allowed to investigate individuals to learn more about their incomes and their pasts. There are also few restrictions on the questions you can ask potential jurors. For example in the O.J. Simpson trial, jurors were asked approximately 290 questions each prior to serving on the jury.

Quebec abolished the right to a jury trial in civil matters. The rationale was that in some cases a jury may not be able to properly review and weigh the evidence and make a determination.

An unknown author in 1899 had this to say on juries: "Few spectacles can be more absurd than that of a jury composed of twelve persons who, without any scientific knowledge or training, are suddenly called upon to adjudicate in controversies in which the most eminent scientific men flatly contradict each other."

Sample Notice to Serve on a Jury

Dear Prospective Juror:

Your name was selected at random from a municipal enumeration list to be considered for inclusion in a Jury Roll, which is a list of potential jurors. The Roll lists the names of citizens resident in a jurisdiction who, if summoned, would be eligible during the ensuing year to serve as jurors.

In order to prepare the Roll, your assistance and cooperation are required. You are required by law to fill out the enclosed questionnaire. Please read each question carefully to ensure that your answer is complete and accurate. Within five days, return the completed questionnaire using the enclosed, pre-addressed, postage-paid envelope.

Please note that receipt of this letter and completion of the questionnaire does not mean that you have actually been chosen to serve on a jury. Your eligibility to serve as a juror will be determined based on the answers you have provided to the questions in the questionnaire.

In conclusion, I want to stress that the jury system is one of the most important elements of our justice system. Jurors are responsible for determining, with the guidance of a judge, questions of fact in either civil or criminal court proceedings. Service as a juror is one of the most valuable contributions members of our society can make.

Thank you for contributing your time to this important endeavour.

Madame, Monsieur,

Nous avons extrait au hasard votre nom d'un recensement municipal en vue de le porter à la liste des jurés. Cette liste comporte les noms de personnes qui résident dans une localité donnée et qui, une fois convoquées, pourraient être admises à faire partie d'un jury au cours des douze prochains mois.

Nous vous saurions gré de bien vouloir nous aider à dresser la liste des jurés en répondant au questionnaire ci-joint, ainsi que la loi l'exige. Veuillez lire attentivement les questions afin d'y apporter des réponses exactes et complètes. Vous êtes prié(e) ensuite de retourner le questionnaire dûment rempli dans les cinq jours suivant sa réception en le glissant dans l'enveloppe pré-affranchie et pré-adressée ci-jointe.

Sachez par ailleurs que le fait de recevoir la présente lettre et de répondre au questionnaire ne veut pas dire que vous avez été effectivement choisi(e) comme juré. Votre admissibilité à faire partie d'un jury sera en effet déterminé d'après vos réponses au questionnaire.

J'aimerais par la même occasion souligner que les proces devant jury constituent l'un des éléments les plus importants dans notre système judiciaire. C'est en effet au jury qu'il incombe, avec l'assistance du juge, de trancher les questions de fait en matière civile ou pénale. Les fonctions de juré comptent parmi les contributions les plus importantes que l'on puisse apporter à la société.

En vous remerciant d'avance du temps que vous consacrerez à cet aspect important de la vie en société, je vous prie de recevoir, Madame/Monsieur, l'expression de mes sentiments distingués.

Sex and the Law

Most people have heard of the President Clinton sex scandal. The first of these sex-related revelations came in a case involving Paula Jones. The revelations crept into our consciousness through articles and commentaries on what had happened and what the press can report when it comes to public figures.

It did not take long for these U.S. issues to take root in Canadian law. The Ontario Court of Appeal recently ruled that the legal test used in the Jones case should be used in Ontario.

The Ontario case involved a group of investors trying to recover losses they suffered when an investment turned sour. A lower court dismissed the investors' case prior to trial. The Court of Appeal reinstated the case, allowing it to be tried.

The court cited Jones vs. Clinton as the proper way to look at serious allegations, be they sex or money issues, prior to a trial. The Ontario court agreed with the U.S. judge's approach in analysing each allegation separately, reviewing the applicable law, looking at the overall picture, and hearing each side's answer to each legal point.

Although it may not be earth shattering and appears to be based on common sense, the law is often slow to incorporate new principles. The legal system is based on written law and judges' comments on that law. Once incorporated into the legal system, the new principle helps people in the future who have similar problems.

The interesting thing is that a Canadian court reached south and drew on a high-profile case to clarify and add to Canadian law. It did so quickly. This did not happen when the O.J. Simpson case was tried. The Clinton case obviously had a greater legal impact.

FROM THE ONTARIO COURT OF APPEAL
IN THE CASE OF DAWSON vs. REXCRAFT
AUGUST 13, 1998, CITING JONES vs. CLINTON

FROM THE JUDGMENT OF MR. JUSTICE BORINS:

[25] The position taken by President Clinton in respect to each of the plaintiff's three claims was identical. He sought to demonstrate the absence of evidence to support at least one element of each of the claims. The plaintiff, in an attempt to survive the motion for summary judgment, adduced evidence to support each element of her claims.

[26] The starting point for Justice Wright in her approach to the motion was to examine each of the plaintiff's claims individually and state the elements of the claim. Then she reviewed the caselaw with respect to each claim for the purpose of determining the range of facts which courts have accepted as establishing the claim. The next step which she took was to examine the entire evidentiary record with a view to determining whether it disclosed a genuine issue for trial with respect to a fact material to the proof of the claim. In the context of the motion before her, President Clinton,

as the moving party, had established that there was no genuine issue for trial by demonstrating an absence of evidence to support the responding party's claims against him. Therefore, to survive the motion for summary judgment, the burden fell on Ms. Jones to adduce evidence which demonstrated that there was evidence which, if accepted by the trier of fact, supported her claims. Wright J. examined this evidence, in the context of the evidentiary record and the elements of the plaintiff's claims as defined by the caselaw, to determine whether the evidence, if accepted by the trier of fact, was capable of proving any, or all, of the claims, and concluded that it was not. President Clinton had succeeded in demonstrating that the plaintiff's claims were undeserving of trial. He had established the absence of a genuine issue for trial in respect to a material fact. In my view, the manner in which Wright J. analyzed the President's motion for summary judgment applies equally to a motion under Ontario Rule 20. It also applies, with suitable modification, to a plaintiff's motion for summary judgment.

Mediation

Given the costs associated with taking a matter to court, the legal system has developed an alternative method of resolving disputes. In some jurisdictions, this alternative system is mandatory before you take a matter to court. It's called **mediation**.

Each party agrees on a government-approved mediator and is responsible for paying the mediator, who receives a written summary of each side's case and convenes the parties to a hearing. After listening to both sides, the mediator often separates them and shuttles between each group in an effort to resolve the dispute.

If the mediator is successful, the case is settled. That's it, it's over. An agreement, called **minutes of settlement**, will be prepared on the spot, and the parties will sign this agreement, thereby ending the lawsuit. There is often an exchange of money in the days that follow, and no court hearing is required.

Mediation works if the parties want to settle. If not the case proceeds to trial.

Q: What is mediation, and how does it fit in the lawsuit?

A: Mediation is the process whereby you and your lawyer, and the person sued and his or her lawyer, try to settle the dispute without a trial. The mediation is held before a third-party mediator agreed to by the lawyers. The mediator will schedule a meeting with the parties to hear both sides of the story and attempt to resolve the conflict. Mediation gives each side a chance to explain its position. If the matter is not settled, the parties go to mediation again before a judicial officer in what is called a **settlement/scheduling conference**. The official will again attempt to reach a resolution, failing which a trial date will be set.

In Ontario, over 95% of all cases are settled before trial. This means fewer than five percent ever make it past the courtroom door. So, in Ontario, a trial lawyer is a rare breed, and those who have had a jury trial are almost extinct.

Q: After an out-of-court settlement, one of the parties began writing letters to various government officials complaining about the legal process. Which recourses are available?

A: An out-of-court settlement usually involves a written agreement whereby one party agrees to stop all legal proceedings or steps against the other party. The agreement also requires all parties to keep matters confidential. It often stipulates that, should any one party breach the agreement, either the settlement monies will have to be paid back or additional monies will have to be paid. The first step is to look at the agreement to determine the terms agreed to by the parties. If, however, there is nothing in the agreement to cover this situation, then the parties can return to court, and a judge can consider issuing a court order preventing the person from writing letters to various officials.

Q: Can minutes of settlement be appealed?

A: Minutes of settlement are another way of saying a settlement agreement was reached. It is usually signed by both parties and properly witnessed. Minutes of settlement imply that the parties have resolved their differences, and it is unlikely that any court would cancel those minutes by any form of appeal, unless one of the parties has been induced to enter into the minutes of settlement by some act of fraud. Fraud will have to be proven convincingly.

**FROM THE ONTARIO SUPERIOR COURT
MEDIATION BROCHURE, OTTAWA,
JANUARY 1997**

*Consider realistically what will happen and what you will do if
you do not settle the case at mediation.*

What are your chances of winning the lawsuit? What are your
chances of losing? What is the best you can hope for in the
lawsuit? What is the wors[t] that can happen to you in the
lawsuit? In between the worst that can happen and the best you
can hope for, what are you likely to win and/or what are you
likely to lose? What are the chances of you having to pay legal
costs to the other party if you lose? How much would you have
to pay? If you win what are your chances of recovering legal
costs from the other side? How much are you likely to recover? If
you are suing someone for money can the other side pay a judgment if you are successful?

What is the financial impact on you of winning or losing? Are
there consequences to losing or winning the lawsuit beyond the
money to be won or lost? Will winning or losing have a moral
or psychological impact? How important is that moral or psychological impact to you? Will the judge's decision create a
precedent that is important to you?

What will it realistically cost to proceed with the lawsuit if it does
not settle at mediation? How much is it going to cost in legal
fees? How long is it likely to take for the lawsuit to be processed
and what effect is that delay likely to have? Will the lawsuit

cause you any stress, embarrassment or publicity? Do you have a relationship with the opposite party or someone else that might be affected by the lawsuit proceeding?

In some cases you may find that you do not have all of the information, documentation or evidence you need to determine what will realistically happen if the lawsuit does not settle (for example, you may find you need an expert's report to determine your chances of win[n]ing or losing the case). If you are in that situation, ask yourself what it is you are missing, how important it is to evaluating the case, how you can best get it, how much time it will take to get it and how much it is likely to cost.

Lawyers and Judges

Lawyers should not ignore the concerns or complaints of clients. Young lawyers anxious for work often take any work that walks in the door, but if the client can't pay, the file may sit for weeks if not months without any activity. Clients who believe that their files are being neglected often complain to provincial law societies, which govern lawyers. The law society will often investigate the complaint and ensure that the client receives the necessary attention.

As a general rule, lawyers should not take cases for which they are not qualified or for which they have no time. Most matters can be dealt with expeditiously so that there are no complaints. Sometimes, however, the delay is caused by the court system and backlogs. If a client does have a legitimate complaint, the lawyer should deal with it and not ignore it.

Clients often complain about the legal fees charged by a lawyer. Lawyers should ensure that they are upfront with clients about the cost involved in a lawsuit. If a client is unhappy, he or she should discuss the account with the lawyer concerned. If they are unable to agree, court officials called **taxing masters or assessment officers,** are available, with an appointment, to review the account in question.

Sometimes the system breaks down, and a judge may be responsible. Judges often make unpopular decisions. That doesn't mean that they are personally responsible. An appeal is the proper route to follow if you disagree with a ruling. If, however, a judge's conduct is at issue, there are professional bodies that can step in to investigate complaints. Clients and lawyers can resort to this complaints process. Be sure, however, to get a second opinion before you launch an attack against a judge.

If you are unhappy with the quality of legal services received, here are some steps to follow.

1. Discuss the problem with your lawyer or an independent adviser.

2. Talk to professional bodies. In Ontario, lawyer complaints can be addressed to the Law Society of Upper Canada at 1-800-668-7380, and judicial complaints anywhere in Canada can be addressed to the Canadian Judicial Council at 112 Kent Street, Suite 450, Ottawa, Ontario, K1A 0W8.

3. If all else fails, consider taking legal action against your lawyer, but note that lawyers have to be sued within six years of the problem.

Q: Can I challenge a lawyer's bill?

A: Yes. Within 30 days of receiving a lawyer's bill, you can challenge it. If you are dissatisfied with the bill, speak to the lawyer concerned and obtain a proper explanation. If the explanation is unsatisfactory, you should write to the lawyer indicating that you wish to formally challenge the bill. If the lawyer refuses to make any changes to it, then — on filing a special form available at most courthouses — the matter goes to court for review. Courts have a judicial officer called a **master** whose job it is to review all legal bills. The master has jurisdiction to hear both sides and review each element of the bill. Once the review is complete, the master renders a decision. At that stage, the bill is upheld, cancelled, or reduced. The client can then pay the revised bill or appeal to a higher court to review the decision of the master.

Q: My lawyer is in jail. Should I review the will that he prepared for me?

A: The answer very much depends on why the lawyer is in jail. If he is in jail for nonpayment of a parking fine, then it is unlikely that he was convicted of an offence relating to his conduct as a lawyer. If, on the other hand, he is in jail due to his actions as a lawyer, then all documents prepared by him should be reviewed. In any event, a will should be reviewed every five years to ensure that it properly reflects your wishes.

Q: How is compensation paid after a successful suit against a lawyer?

A: All lawyers carry professional liability insurance. This means that an insurance company has insured the lawyer for professional misconduct. If a ruling has found the lawyer guilty, then the insurance company will pay the amount in question. If the insurance company refuses to pay and all appeals have been exhausted, then the insurance company itself can be taken to court for failure to pay. This second lawsuit will be serious enough to warrant a court's imposing severe penalties on the insurance company, which penalties will probably include full compensation for your legal fees.

Q: If one lawyer is negligent, are his or her partners also responsible?

A: This very much depends on what the lawyer was doing. If the lawyer acted as a representative of the law firm, then all the partners are responsible. If, on the other hand, the lawyer acted independently, then his or her partners may not be responsible.

Lawyers send letters for clients demanding this or that be done. In one case, a young lawyer demanded payment for unpaid funeral services. He used a standard form letter for defective car parts. The letter to the grieving family therefore demanded payment, "failing which, the parts will be returned to you." The family was not amused, but it paid.

Q: A client wants to recover monies through the law society insurance fund. How does the client go about claiming from that fund?

A: Most provincial law societies have funds available to compensate clients who have been wronged through the actions of lawyers in the respective province. An individual who believes that he or she has suffered damages as a result of a lawyer's actions sets out the complaint in writing and forwards it to the law society. The law society then reviews the complaint and often meets with the concerned client. If the claim is established, the law society representative advances it on behalf of the client and makes sure that the client is paid.

Q: After a lengthy legal battle, an individual wishes to sue the judges and lawyers concerned due to delays encountered in the legal system. Can the individual sue?

A: Judges, and in some cases lawyers, are immune from lawsuits for actions that occur within a courtroom. It is up to the judge presiding over the trial to ensure that it is dealt with expeditiously. Courts are slowly chipping away at backlogs in an effort to streamline the legal process. There is little an individual can do about delays that are an inherent part of the current system.

Q: A judge suggested that a jury find the accused person guilty of a certain criminal charge. The jury found otherwise. Are there grounds for appeal?

A: The jury are the ultimate triers of fact, and, if they make a ruling that goes against the judge's recommendations, only in very limited circumstances can the judge set aside that ruling. Otherwise, the ruling of the jury stands since they are the triers of fact. Appeals are often based on the instructions that a judge gave to the jury prior to their deliberations. A review of the judge's instructions would determine whether there are grounds for appeal.

Q: How do I complain about a judge?

A: Judges are governed by a professional association called the **Canadian Judicial Council**, and all complaints can be directed to it. The complaint is investigated and may result in a hearing on the judge's conduct.

Lawyers

When lawyers go to court, they wear black robes that remind some of the dress worn by nineteenth-century highwaymen. While lawyers might be considered to rob clients with the legal fees they charge, the robes themselves are steeped in history.

Courts were originally created as a branch of the church. The reason was twofold. First, the clergy were thought to be the only literate and educated class able to carry forth the law. Second, it was thought that only the clergy could put the fear of God into witnesses so that the truth would come out at a trial. The clergy of the day wore black robes similar to those still seen today in many churches.

The kings and queens of Europe saw that the church-run courts made money. In those days, you bought the right to sue. The saying was "If you have a writ, you have a right, and with a right a remedy." In plain language, if the rights you had were defined and violated, you could sue and win. One purchased the right to sue. The costs of these "rights" generated money for the church and monarchy.

In response, royalty created their own set of "rights" and as a result generated revenues. They also needed "lawyers" to help them collect on these rights. Again, this class of individuals dressed as the courtiers of the day dressed. Early judicial dress had leggings, wigs, and fancy shoes as worn in and about the royal palace. Lawyers then placed the black robes over this fancy dress.

Eventually, the two court systems merged, as did the dress of lawyers. Rights have now been broadened by laws that anyone can use. The "fee" to sue is now a government stamp for which one has to pay when a lawsuit is started. Yet the dress of lawyers remains, though it has been modified. They no longer wear leggings, but they still wear black robes.

The robes have pieces of cloth that run from the shoulder to midway down the back. Once a purse hung from that piece of cloth. A prospective client would put coins into that pouch. The lawyer, who would never be seen in public counting the money, would flip the cloth and purse to the front and peer into the pouch. If the coins were sufficient, the lawyer would take your case. If not, the pouch would be flipped back, and the coins would spill onto the earthen floor for all to see (and no doubt grab). That was the custom. To this day in England, the lawyer who goes to court (a **barrister**) usually has another lawyer (a **solicitor**) collect the money, so the tradition of not being seen to touch a client's money remains.

The term "solicitor" originated from this money-collecting exercise. The legacy lives on whenever you see the sign "No Soliciting" on public buildings. People who go around getting business are soliciting customers or clients. Lawyers are no different.

The barrister was so called because he or she was able to approach the **bar**. In the old courts, the public was segregated from the lawyers and judges, usually at a distance beyond which a rotten tomato could be flung. The lawyers who pleaded a case could approach the bar and sometimes stand on the other side, for it was assumed that they would not throw tomatoes, only verbal barbs.

A **Queen's Counsel** was allowed to stand closer to the bench where the judge would sit and wore a different robe made of silk without that band of cloth. Originally, the QC was paid directly from the royal treasury. Silk was reserved for judges and the upper nobility, and by being named a QC one was approaching that status and hence could dress like them.

Wigs were originally used to hide fleas and lice and the powder put on heads to kill those pests. This tradition soon fell by the wayside when lawyers realized that washing their hair also killed the little critters. So, though lawyers still look like high-waymen with those black robes (an old tradition) and still take your money (a continuing tradition), they are now thoroughly modern because they bathe.

Methods of Paying for Legal Services

In today's competitive market, law firms offer their clients various alternatives to pay for legal services. Traditionally, lawyers charge by the hour, which means that, if a case takes some time to resolve, legal fees can eat up much of the ultimate award.

Most law firms offer alternative billing strategies tailored to a client's needs. Here are some of the options.

1. *Monthly retainer*: This is a set amount that a client pays on a monthly basis regardless of the hours spent.

2. *Contingency*: The contingency fee is compensation based on the amount received at the end of a legal dispute.

3. *Flat fee*: This is negotiated between the firm and the client. An amount is paid for a set number of hours or for a certain task.

4. *Task-based billing*: Under this system, a budget is established against which bills are rendered. When the set amount is reached, a new amount is determined for future work.

5. *Blended rates*: A rate is set for senior lawyers, and a lower fee is set for junior lawyers. The senior lawyer supervises the junior lawyer, who carries out much of the work and charges a lower hourly rate for the time spent on the case.

6. *Result-driven fees*: A minimum amount is charged up front, with the bulk of the legal fees charged when the matter is resolved. A cap of approximately 20% is set for the lawyer's compensation based on results achieved.

There are many alternatives to the traditional hourly billing system, and they should be discussed and agreed to by you and your lawyer.

Private Meetings with Judges

In today's competitive environment, lawyers sometimes try to win a case at any cost. This includes pushing opposing counsel around in court (with verbal barbs).

Many a TV series has shown one lawyer or another meeting privately with a judge in order to resolve a conflict. In the Canadian justice system, this is not condoned. A lawyer cannot meet with a judge in a private session since so doing may be perceived as influencing the case. All meetings must be held with all lawyers present and in some cases the clients. Private meetings should not take place, nor should a lawyer engage in a letter-writing campaign with the presiding judge.

FROM THE ONTARIO SUPERIOR COURT IN THE CASE OF WEI vs. DALES JANUARY 22, 1988

FROM THE JUDGMENT OF CHADWICK J.:

There is a growing trend by some counsel to try and improve their position or intimidate other counsel by corresponding directly with the judiciary.

With the many changes in court administration and especially with implementation of case management there is obviously going to be more direct communication between the judiciary and the bar. However, if this is to take place then caution must be used so that only administrative matters which are in issue are addressed and the correspondence is not used in an attempt to prejudice the mind of the judge or to be used at a later date in attempt to disqualify that judge from hearing a particular case.

Discharging a Lawyer

A lawyer is hired to advance your rights or protect your interests. A judge is meant to rule on the merits of your case. On rare occasions, the system breaks down, and then there is an outcry.

Sometimes, lawyers have problems advancing a client's interest because they have a problem either with the client or with the court system. In that case, the best alternative is to have the lawyer withdraw from the case so that a new lawyer can get involved. Doing so often eliminates road blocks.

FROM MANITOBA
IN THE CASE OF R. vs. SWARTZ
(1977) 34 CCC (2d) 477

FROM THE JUDGMENT OF CHIEF JUSTICE FREEDMAN:

Sometimes counsel cannot divert the judge from a course of conduct, which makes it very difficult for him to discharge his duties and renders it impossible for his client to have a fair trial. In those cases, courageous counsel have sometimes withdrawn from the case and walked out of court in protest. The traditions of the Bar do not exclude such an extreme measure. The following ruling was given by the Bar Council in 1933:

> "If counsel is unfairly interfered with to such an extent as to defeat the course of justice it may be necessary for counsel to withdraw from the case or to leave the matter to be dealt with on appeal. Counsel should always remember that his paramount duty is to protect the interest of his client. Naturally, this measure has been taken by counsel only in exceptional cases."

In the case, in 1928, before Lord Hewart, L.C.J., mentioned above, Serjeant Sullivan walked out in protest from the court of Lord Hewart. His action is usually referred to with approval by fellow barristers.

Survey

A 1998 Angus Reid Group public opinion poll showed that doctors, police officers, and teachers tend to receive more respect than journalists, lawyers, and politicians. The survey ranked professions as follows, from best to worst: doctors, police officers, teachers, priests, judges, artists, journalists, lawyers, labour leaders, and politicians. Are lawyers moving ever so slightly up the "food chain"?

Judges

The appointment of judges to the Supreme Court of Canada is within the purview of the prime minister. Prior to the mid-1970s, there was little if any outside consultation on appointments. Thereafter, the system was changed to include input from chief judges, provincial attorneys general, and the Canadian Bar Association. A select few candidates have the stature and qualifications to meet the demands of being a Supreme Court judge, the highest judicial office. Many refuse to be considered because they make more money in private practice. There are also social restrictions with the appointment, as judges in Ottawa can't socialize with politicians or lawyers who appear in the Supreme Court.

Some people have suggested that there should be public hearings to review all candidates. Others have suggested that a judge's personal view on a subject is irrelevant since judges decide cases based on the facts and legal arguments presented. A judgment often goes one way or another depending on the input of lawyers.

Our judicial system has checks and balances in the form of public outcry or parliamentary action. If a judge goes too far off on a tangent, public criticism may lead to parliamentary censure and, as a last resort, removal by Parliament. There is also the Canadian Judicial Council, a professional body that oversees the training and discipline of judges. Complaints can be submitted by anyone, and all matters are investigated.

The system can be improved, but it works. Judgments from the Supreme Court are well reasoned and researched. The judges have research staffs that are the envy of all other judges and all lawyers.

In France, there is a separate school system for judges. If you want to be a judge, you go to judges' school and make your way into the judicial system through specialized training. In the United States, some judges are elected. Perhaps Canadians can learn from these other systems and incorporate the best ideas from abroad to improve on our own system of judging.

FROM A BROCHURE PUBLISHED BY THE CANADIAN JUDICIAL COUNCIL MAY 2000

Every year Canada's federally appointed judges make hundreds of thousands of decisions on matters that range from procedural questions to the most basic interests of those appearing before them.

Judges can make mistakes. When one side or the other in a legal dispute thinks that the judge has come to the *wrong decision*, our system of justice allows that person to appeal the decision to a higher court. Appeal courts can reverse or vary decisions of other judges. The fact that an appeal court has overturned a judge's decision does not mean that the judge's conduct was improper.

Whether judges are correct or incorrect in their decisions, a high standard of personal conduct is expected of them. When someone believes that a judge's *behaviour is of serious concern*, or that a judge is not fit to be on the bench, here too our system of justice provides a remedy. In this case a complaint may be made to the Canadian Judicial Council.

An important difference

The distinction between *decisions* and *conduct* is fundamental.

Issue	Remedy
A judge's *decision* is questioned	Review of the *decision* by a higher court — appeal
A judge's *conduct* is questioned	Review of the *conduct* by the Canadian Judicial Council — complaint

The complaints process

It is open to you to make a written complaint if you believe that a judge's conduct is improper, on or off the bench, including conduct toward anyone involved in a case before that judge.

There are no required forms. You need not be represented by a lawyer. There are no prescribed deadlines. There is no cost to you.

The Council examines every complaint seriously, conscientiously, and as promptly as possible.

The process is open and accessible to everyone, whatever their knowledge of the legal system, skill, status, position or financial resources. The Council takes care to be fair to everyone involved. Given that judges sometimes have to make unpopular decisions, the Council tries to establish whether complaints about judges are well-founded.

Suing Other Entities

There is a popular misconception that you can't sue professionals. This is not true. All professionals are responsible to their customers or clients if they make mistakes. These errors of judgment can form the subject of a lawsuit if you as the client relied on this professional.

If, for example, you are a neophyte in investing and you hire a broker, that broker will have to sit down with you to determine your needs and your financial means. If she does her job and the market crashes, she may not be held responsible. If, on the other hand, you told her to invest your money in safe government bonds and she invested it in risky stocks, then she may be held responsible if the market crashes. This is so because she failed to follow your instructions and thereby to protect your money.

Similarly, municipalities can be sued if they act unfairly in assessing taxes. School boards and provincial premiers are not immune from lawsuits. They may have a defence if they can prove that they acted in the public interest, but if a premier or schoolteacher hits you with a car, or commits any personal act against you, like any other citizen he or she can be sued.

Brokers

Q: An individual is concerned about a potential conflict of interest when a broker trades privately in shares that he recommended for purchase. What options are available?

A: If a broker engages in trades while standing in a conflict-of-interest position, the matter should be raised with the brokerage branch office in question. Most brokerage houses have conflict-of-interest departments where internal investigators review questionable trades. You can also raise concerns with the Investment Dealers Association, which would also investigate the matter and, if necessary, persuade the brokerage house to resolve the complaint.

> Brokers must respect the "know your client" rule. This rule means that they have to sit down with clients and find out all about their financial limits, stock market experience, and future goals. If they do not, they may be liable for future losses in your brokerage account.

Q: What do I do if money is missing from my brokerage account?

A: The first step is to raise the issue with the broker or the branch in question. You may also contact the head office. If you don't receive a satisfactory response or compensation, you should raise your concerns with the Investment Dealers Association, the professional body governing all brokers. If all else fails, you will have to hire a lawyer and sue the broker.

Q: An individual opened an account with a major brokerage house, completed a "know your client" form, and clearly indicated that he didn't want high-risk stocks or bonds. Yet the broker didn't heed the wishes of the investor, and eventually the money was lost. What can be done?

A: The investor obviously received poor advice and guidance, and the broker didn't respect the "know your client" form. Brokers must invest in items that are suitable given the person's age, background, and risk tolerance. The broker would therefore be liable for the losses incurred. Recently, the Supreme Court of Canada confirmed this principle in a case involving an elderly person who'd given life savings to a broker who, over time, lost the entire portfolio.

Q: Can I recover money if I approach a professional association instead of going through the civil courts?

A: Individuals can often recover money through professional associations and avoid the expense of courtroom litigation. Winning depends on the nature of the claim and the amount of documentation available to support it. It also depends on the association in question. For example, the Investment Dealers Association of Canada (for stockbrokers) has a system of mediation meant to avoid the court system yet provide recourse to have complaints heard and compensation awarded.

Municipalities

Q: How do I challenge a tax assessment?

A: When you receive a tax assessment, you are provided with information on how to contest that assessment. Generally, you are required to set out your objection within a set period of time. Often a hearing is convened, and you are required to attend it and explain why you are challenging the assessment. The hearing will then determine the amount you are required to pay.

Q: What restrictions exist on suing a municipality?

A: There are strict laws as to when a municipality can be sued. In particular, slips on sidewalks and nonrepair of roads require the person injured to give formal notice of the intention to sue within a very short time frame. This notice period may be as short as five days and as long as 10 days. Once the proper notice has been given, the lawsuit follows the normal course of a claim, a defence, questioning, and a trial.

Q: Can I sue a municipality for pain and suffering and time wasted by bureaucrats?

A: No. Delays are part of our system of government. Unless you can show that the delay was intentional and directed toward you personally, versus a delay that occurs with everyone else in the municipality, your right to sue doesn't exist.

Q: How do I contest a traffic ticket without a lawyer?

A: When you receive a traffic ticket, you are required to return the ticket to the municipal authorities by checking a box indicating whether you are guilty or not guilty. If you choose the "not guilty" option, you will be notified by the municipal court (in the jurisdiction in which the ticket was issued) of a hearing date. You will then attend that hearing with supporting documents and witnesses to contest the ticket before a judge. The judge will then render a decision finding you either guilty or not guilty based on the evidence presented.

Two municipal workers were clearing a sewer. A homeowner was experiencing problems with a toilet that would not flush. The homeowner assumed that the problem was caused by the municipal workers. They were asked to take a look and kindly complied. The workers removed the main drain plug in the basement of the house. As there had been an accumulation of flushing and therefore pressure, the plug rose like a gusher, and the workers were covered in sewage. They were not happy and left the house via the living room and not the back door. In the subsequent court action, the workers were fined $50 each for nuisance (they did not have to walk on the living room carpet), and the municipality was held blameless for damages to the house because all it was doing was cleaning the sewer.

Q: How do I represent myself in municipal court when the party being sued is a lawyer?

A: If you have thoroughly investigated the facts and have all the witnesses lined up in order to prove those facts in a court of law, the judge will assist you in presenting your case. You should not be intimidated if the party being sued is a lawyer, since he or she is acting in a personal capacity and not as a lawyer. The judge will ensure that there is fairness all around.

Private Schools

Q: Certain incidents occurred in a private school. Can the parents sue?

A: Whenever problems arise, whether in the public or the private system, the school administration (including the private school's board of directors) should be contacted, failing which the issue should be raised with the Ministry of Education. All schools in the province are subject to the rules and regulations set out by the ministry. Only as a last recourse should a lawsuit be considered. In that event, parents have to balance the issue of enforcing their rights with a child's continued education at that institution.

School Boards

Q: Can I sue a school board?

A: Any legal entity, be it a person or a corporation, can be sued. Immunity from lawsuits is rare in our society, and generally anyone can be sued if he or she does something that is illegal or improper.

Premiers

Q: Can I sue a provincial premier?

A: Anyone can be sued provided the legal proceedings are brought to his or her attention by hand delivering a copy of the lawsuit. Premiers or prime ministers may argue that what was allegedly done occurred within the rules governing their office. Thus, they would be exempt from a lawsuit. On the other hand, if they acted outside that authority, they may be liable.

CHAPTER TWO

Individual Rights

Individuals come up against banks, stores, airlines, and other entities on a day-to-day basis. Occasionally, problems arise; you may buy a loaf of bread and take it home only to find out that half of it has gone mouldy. Your choice is then to throw the loaf out and vow never to purchase bread from that store again or take the bread back and get a refund or replacement. This clash between enforcing your rights and leaving matters as they are frequently occurs.

Perhaps you are a tenant in an apartment building and your faucet leaks. You can either do the minor repair yourself or call the building superintendent. If you call the superintendent for every single thing that goes wrong within your apartment, you might be viewed as a nuisance, and, when it comes to renewing your lease, you might not be able to renew it on satisfactory terms. The choice is therefore to do the repairs yourself or call the superintendent. The same applies to the law; you can sue or move on.

In the area of consumer protection, the laws have changed over the years. Gone are the days when it was always "buyer beware." Not only are consumers more cautious, but also merchants deliver better service due to competition and perhaps the threat of lawsuits. Sometimes problems remain, especially when it comes to repairing high-tech goods or renovating a home.

With the advent of the Canadian Charter of Rights and Freedoms, courts focus on rights that we all have as members of society. Charter rights must always remain paramount when individuals clash with society and its institutions. Unfortunately, we cannot deal with all charter issues, for they would form the basis of a separate book.

We will begin this chapter on individual rights by focusing on consumer issues such as whether a store is required to sell a good at the advertised price (yes) and whether a verbal contract is enforceable in court (also yes). We will then cover issues between neighbours, a frequent source of litigation. Municipal issues are covered given the recent Supreme Court of Canada ruling that local municipalities may be held partially liable for faulty home renovations. Car accidents and insurance are also discussed, followed by issues surrounding individual legal responsibility. We will touch on health issues and on financial/banking matters.

These questions have come from clients and CBC radio listeners. I hope to provide some basic information that will help to explain the law and save you time should you need to consult with a lawyer.

Consumers

Q: Is a store required to sell an item for the advertised price?

A: Yes. If the price is clear and without conditions, the store must sell the item for that price. If it refuses to do so, you can contact a government agency (e.g., the Department of Consumer and Corporate Affairs, Canada), which will enforce the law in this matter.

Q: An individual was unable to use a seat-sale ticket, which had been issued as nonrefundable. What recourse is available?

A: If the ticket is clear on its face, the money paid will be lost. If there was a good reason for nonuse, such as a sudden medical condition, the airline may make an exception if the right medical proof is provided.

Q: What can I do if a mail-order product is defective?

A: You should first try to return and exchange the product. If that option is not available, you can sue the company or complain to the Department of Consumer and Corporate Affairs, Canada.

Q: An individual won a contest and arranged with the supplier to substitute the prize for one of equal value. No prize has been delivered. What can be done?

A: First, the winner should get a letter from the contest organizers clearly indicating that he or she has won the contest. Second, with that letter, the winner should write to the supplier confirming that a substitute prize should have been awarded. The winner should then ask that it be delivered. If the supplier refuses, an alternative is to contact the media. Since the contest organizers and the supplier will not want adverse publicity, they will probably deliver the prize immediately. If they refuse, then as a last resort the matter can be taken to court.

Q: Do I have to pay for a VCR or computer repair bill when the work is faulty?

A: If the work is faulty, you can withhold payment until the machine works. Generally, you should try to sort things out with the repair person before you consider suing for faulty workmanship.

Q: A customer at a drive-through had her drink spill in her car. The spill leaked into the drive shaft of the car, causing major damage. This was discovered after the car left the premises. Can the customer sue the drive-through?

A: There have been many cases of customers being burned by hot coffee and restaurants being held liable. In a similar way, the soft drink caused extensive damage to the car, and the customer should be compensated. Unfortunately, the customer did not bring this problem immediately to the manager's attention and now requires a written opinion from a mechanic indicating that the source of the damage was the spilled drink. The manager should be shown this letter. If the company is willing to pay for the repairs, then the problem is solved. If not, then it becomes a question of whether the mechanic and customer will be believed (was it the fault of the customer or the drive-though?) when the matter goes to court.

The Fine Print

Do you ever read the fine print on an airline ticket? Do you ever read the first few pages of your phone book? Both your airline ticket and the phone book limit liability on behalf of the airline and the telephone companies. If your luggage is lost, you may not be entitled to recover every penny, since there is a limit printed on your ticket. If you experience problems with your telephone, your compensation is also limited.

One individual wished to sue a major phone book publisher for having printed his unlisted number. He wanted anonymity, which disappeared with the printing of his name, address, and phone number. Although he was entitled to sue, the fine print in the front of the phone book limited liability to the greater of $20 or three times his monthly bill. Not much consolation for someone who would have to move in order to maintain anonymity.

Manufacturers' Warnings

Manufacturers print warnings on everything from clothing to appliances. These warnings are there so that, if they are sued, they can always point to the warning labels in an effort to absolve themselves from liability.

As most people know, dishwashers are designed so that the cutlery tray is at the front of the machine. Recently, a British coroner was called to investigate the death of a child who'd fallen on a cutlery tray and had a knife pierce his chest. Suggestions for change included a special compartment so that knives can be loaded horizontally and cutlery trays in the back of the dishwasher. Don't be surprised if you see labels appearing on dishwashers that state "Danger, keep children away from this machine. It may cause injury."

Contracts

Q: An individual did some work on a fixed-price contract, received partial payment, and is now owed money. What can be done?

A: Since the price was set and agreed to, the other party owes the balance unless there is some reason for nonpayment, such as defective work. If the work was properly done, then the item can be seized with a court order, or a lien can be placed on the item. A lien binds the item so that a subsequent buyer has to pay the debt before he or she becomes the new owner free and clear of previous debts.

Q: Should an independent building cleaner continue working after a mortgage holder takes over the property?

A: Since the cleaning contract was signed with the owner, who defaulted in paying her mortgage debt, the cleaner should ensure that the mortgage company wants him to continue with the upkeep of the property. Otherwise, he may work for naught.

With the fall of communism in many countries, new groups of officials took over overseas management of these countries' affairs. In one case, the new officials had much trouble understanding that in Canada you pay first and then take delivery of the item in question. They were led to believe that you used the item first, and, if you were satisfied with it, then you paid for it. This belief caused great delays in real estate transactions as these new officials learned all about Canadian real estate practices.

Q: Is a verbal contract enforceable in a court of law?

A: Generally, yes, if the terms can be proven in court. If you have witnesses and some evidence that the contract was carried out in part, then you can prove the contract and win the lawsuit. If it's one person's word against another's, then it becomes a question of who makes a more credible witness.

Q: A contractor agreed to a fixed-price contract and invoiced for a larger amount. There was then a claim by a subcontractor for nonpayment. How do I sort out these competing interests?

A: The subcontractor has to be paid. If there is a balance due to the main contractor, you can deduct the amount you pay to the subcontractor. As for the fixed-price contract, a contract is a contract, and unless you agreed to the overrun in price you are not responsible for the excess.

Q: An annual fee was paid for road maintenance on a cottage property. The road is now privately managed. Is the fee still due?

A: When the original agreement for purchase of the cottage was made, there may have been a condition requiring a contribution to road maintenance regardless of who does the work. If not, then it's up to each new party to negotiate a deal. At the end of the day, if you want the road maintained, someone will have to be paid for the work.

Q: A parent in Canada wishes to give a piano to a child who lives in the United States. Does the parent have to communicate with U.S. Customs before the piano arrives at the border, or can the piano be shipped without preclearance?

A: The parent should prepare a signed piece of paper indicating that the piano (with a precise description of it) is a gift to the child, who now lives in the United States. With this paper, the parent can either transport the piano or have a mover transport it without any duties or taxes paid at the border. The parent should make extra copies of the letter in case the Customs officer wishes to keep a copy.

Q: A contractor required a customer to sign a contract indicating that the customer waived all provincial and municipal laws applicable to the renovation. Is this valid?

A: This type of clause is called a "waiver," and for it to be effective it must be clearly brought to the customer's attention. It must also meet certain standards. One cannot waive the application of laws that are of general benefit to everyone. The clause in this case would not be effective.

Q: As a result of faulty concrete work, a homeowner has withheld half of the payment due to the contractor. The contractor is now threatening to bring a lawsuit. What can the homeowner do?

A: The homeowner has the right to withhold payment until the work is done properly. If the contractor fails to repair the concrete, then the homeowner can have another company undertake the repairs and use the money held back to pay the new company.

Q: A 15-year-old house began to crack, and the homeowner discovered that no permits were issued for the original work. Who would be held liable in this situation?

A: If the work was clearly improperly done, and no permits were issued, then previous owners would be liable as well as the contractor and/or the city for failure to properly construct or inspect the house.

Q: A 29-year-old roof has begun to leak. Can the homeowner sue the contractor or the city for the cost of repairs?

A: If the city inspected and approved installation of the roof, then it may be jointly liable with the contractor if subsequent problems arise. This is subject, however, to the homeowner's proving that the work was not properly done and that the damages have been caused by something other than normal wear and tear and age. Along with these principles is the issue that you must sue within a reasonable period of time, and 29 years may be outside that period.

Q: A company for which I did contract work has shut down without paying me. What are my options?

A: You may argue that you were in fact an employee and should be covered by provincial wage laws. Or you may make a claim in bankruptcy court if that option was chosen by the company. You may even consider suing the directors or officers of the company since they may have personal liability for employees, if you qualify.

Q: Can I get out of a contract on the basis of false statements?

A: If you entered into the contract based on certain statements or representations, you may be able to have the contract cancelled on that basis. Much will depend on proof of the statements made.

Low Bids

One would think that, if yours was the lowest bid for contract work or the highest bid at an auction, you'd be awarded the contract or sold the item. That is not always the case. Many auctions and bid requests clearly state that the owner has the absolute right to reject any bid or offer. As long as this condition is clearly stated at the outset, the owner can do as he or she pleases. If, however, the owner acts in an arbitrary manner, then he or she can be forced to make a contract with you, sell you the item, or at least pay you damages.

Municipalities

The Supreme Court of Canada recently ruled that a municipality may be liable to a homeowner if it approves a renovation that later turns out badly. The case in question involved a new foundation that later sagged. The inspector had given an okay when in fact the underpinnings for the foundation were insufficient. The Supreme Court ruled that the contractor and the city can be held jointly responsible if the damages were foreseeable and if the city decided to inspect buildings. When a municipal authority decides to regulate a certain activity and fails to properly regulate that activity, it can be held liable.

Although the case involved a home renovation, the same comments can apply to restaurants. If the city inspects restaurants for health and safety concerns, it assumes part of the responsibility if something goes wrong. This is not to say that municipalities are to be considered like insurance companies. If they fail to take adequate steps and you have acted reasonably, they may be held liable.

Neighbours

Q: A neighbour's renovations have caused debris to leech into my property. What can be done?

A: Renovations must be done promptly and efficiently without causing damage to one's neighbours. The first recourse is to contact city inspectors to have them inspect the site and force the homeowner to undertake the repairs quickly. If the city refuses to do so, then you can sue your neighbour for damages caused to your property and interference with the enjoyment of your property.

Q: A neighbour is doing his own home renovations and causing excessive noise. What can I do?

A: Again, the local municipality has the right to prevent nuisances from being caused to neighbours and may well have a noise by-law in place. If the noise over a period of time exceeds the by-law limits, the municipality can restrict when the renovations are done and the level of noise.

Q: We have used a neighbouring farm property for a decade, but the land was sold and fenced off. Can the new owner do that?

A: Yes. The farmer is entitled to fence the property and use it for farming. If a neighbour has been using the property without permission, then that use must stop. Squatter's rights cannot be acquired by 10 years of use.

Q: How can I stop someone from trespassing on my property?

A: There are two simple ways, the first being to erect a fence, and the second being to post a sign. The sign provides notice to any trespassers that, if they cross the fence or ignore the sign, they can be forcibly removed by the appropriate authorities and/or be sued for trespass.

Landlords and Repairs

When your faucet leaks, you have the right to complain and have your landlord fix it. If you become a nuisance and have every single broken thing fixed by the landlord, when it comes time to renew your lease the landlord may not be keen on renewing it. There is a fine line between exerting your rights and doing the repairs yourself to maintain goodwill in the relationship.

In one case, however, a building fell into serious disrepair. The sauna did not work. A resident went into it and felt quite comfortable as the heat increased. Unfortunately, the thermostat was broken, and the heat kept rising. When this occurs, the body tends to relax and often falls asleep. The tenant fell asleep, only to be discovered two days later. He had died. Given 250°F of heat over two days, you can well imagine what had happened to the body.

Insurance Coverage

A homeowner attempted to fix a gas connection. All the fixtures appeared to have been properly connected, but the outside valve had not been properly installed or checked. When the homeowner went outside to take a cigarette break, he and the trailer exploded. The question was whether the insurance company for the trailer would have to provide coverage. The court held that it would since the man had no way of knowing for sure that the outside connection was faulty.

Cars

Q: What recourses are available for problems with a rental car that needs to be towed?

A: If the car you are renting breaks down, and if the rental agreement clearly specifies that towing costs will be paid in a set area, then you cannot claim towing charges outside that area. On the other hand, if a mechanic finds that the car was not roadworthy, you may be able to cancel the rental agreement or claim compensation for expenses caused by the breakdown of the car.

Q: I paid a mechanic up front to repair my car motor, but he did not complete the work. What can be done?

A: Demand that the work be done by a set date. If the date comes and goes without the repairs being made, you can have the motor repaired elsewhere. You would then sue the original repair shop for the inconvenience and to recover your lost money.

Q: An individual who unknowingly backed into another car was later charged with leaving the scene of an accident and fingerprinted. Why did she have to be fingerprinted?

A: If you are charged under the Criminal Code, you have to be fingerprinted before going to court. If you plead guilty, records are kept. If you plead not guilty and win, the records can be destroyed. As for the charge of leaving the scene of an accident, under the Criminal Code an individual is guilty of that offence only if he or she had the intention of leaving the scene of the accident. If an individual did not realize an accident had occurred, then he or she did not have the necessary intention in leaving it. The police can also charge a person under the Highway Traffic Act for the same offence. Under this act, there is no need for fingerprinting, there is no criminal record, and the penalty is less severe.

Q: A car parked in a shopping-centre lot marked "For Customers Only" was towed away because the driver left the premises. Is this legal?

A: When you park your car, you are on someone's property, in this case the mall owner's property. The rule is that you can park only if you shop at the mall. The security people obviously observed the individual leaving the lot and had the car impounded. It is unfortunate, but legally speaking the car was trespassing on the property.

Q: A car repaired in one province was involved in an accident in another province due to the faulty repair. What can be done?

A: In areas that have no-fault insurance programs, your insurance company has to sue to recover losses incurred. If you have the right to sue under your policy, then that option is open to you, and you can sue in the jurisdiction in which you live.

The Demerit Point System

In Ontario, if you are charged with an offence under the Highway Traffic Act, you get demerit points. Too many points lead to the loss of your licence. After two years, these points are wiped out. Here is a sample list of offences.

Points   Offence

2
- failing to ensure that a passenger under 16 is wearing a seatbelt
- failing to ensure that a passenger less than 23 kg is properly secured
- failing to wear your seatbelt
- reversing on a divided high-speed road
- unnecessary slow driving
- failing to signal
- making improper right and left turns
- failing to share the road
- failing to stop at a pedestrian crossing
- failing to obey signs
- towing people — on toboggans, bicycles, etc.
- making prohibited turns
- improperly opening your vehicle's door
- failing to lower your headlight beam

3
- crossing a divided road where no proper crossing is provided
- driving or operating a vehicle on a closed road
- going the wrong way on a one-way road
- crowding the driver's seat
- improperly driving/passing where road is divided into lanes
- failing to report a collision to police
- driving the wrong way on a divided road
- failing to obey the directions of a police officer
- failing to obey a stop sign, traffic signal, or railway-crossing signal
- failing to yield the right-of-way
- driving through, around, or under a railway-crossing barrier
- exceeding the speed limit by 16 to 29 km/hr

4
- following too closely
- exceeding the speed limit by 30 to 49 km/hr

5
- driver of a bus failing to stop at an unprotected crossing

6
- failing to stop for a school bus
- exceeding the speed limit by 50 km/hr or more
- racing
- careless driving

7
- failing to remain at the scene of a collision

Insurance

Q: My insurance company has lost all records of my coverage. What can I do?

A: If you have copies of insurance policies and premium payments, then the insurance company will likely honour the contract. If, however, the company refuses to grant any form of coverage, then the only alternative is to sue it. The court will likely declare that the insurance policy was valid and order that payment be made.

Q: How does one settle a claim in Ontario for a car accident in British Columbia involving an Ontario driver?

A: Ontario has a system of no-fault insurance. Under this system, all accidents are reported to the insurance company of each driver, and the drivers settle the claim between the companies. If a lawsuit is required against a resident of another province, the insurance company will take over the case and attempt to recover any necessary payment.

Q: A driver changed car-insurance companies but just prior to the change had an accident under the old insurance policy. Was the driver required to disclose the accident?

A: Yes. Failure to disclose previous accidents would entitle the new insurance company to cancel coverage. It is far better to have insurance coverage with a higher premium (due to the risk of accidents) than to risk no coverage at all because you failed to disclose an important fact.

Q: An individual had a car accident and was told by his insurance company that the premium would not increase because he was not at fault. But conflicting statements in the police report indicated split responsibility, so the company increased the rate after all. Can anything be done?

A: An individual has a year from when the accident occurred to sort out the problems caused by the accident. If possible, statements from the police officer(s) should be obtained either directly or through a lawyer. These statements should be provided to the insurance company so that it can reconsider the increased premiums.

Q: An individual, hit from behind in a car accident and not at fault, has a dispute with her insurance company about payment for repairs.

A: In Ontario, all drivers are covered by a no-fault insurance scheme, and the right to sue in most cases has been taken away. Car values are determined by industry guidelines, and, if a driver disagrees with the amount of the settlement, he or she can challenge the insurance company by way of either arbitration or court action. The driver will have to prove that the car was being used in a proper manner.

Q: Are premiums increased with a history of accidents?

A: Generally, insurance companies will increase your premiums if you have a history of accidents. If you have not owned a car, and have no other history of accidents, the insurance company will take that into account in adjusting premiums.

Q: Should I get extra insurance if I intend to make frequent trips to the United States?

A: Liability for accidents in the United States far exceeds the amounts courts award in Canada. If an individual travels frequently to the United States, additional insurance protection should be obtained through the individual's insurance company.

Q: Should out-of-province insurance be obtained when short-term employment requires a change of residence?

A: Your insurance broker should be contacted to determine whether your policy covers you when you move from one province to another. Alternatively, you can review the insurance contract itself to see if it contains conditions on residency. If there are conditions, then you should obtain additional coverage.

Q: What recourse is available to a person who dropped insurance coverage after selling a car to go to university, then decided to purchase a car only to discover that the company wanted to charge a higher-than-average premium because he had no current insurance history?

A: If an individual can prove that he or she has had a history of insurance coverage (without accidents) prior to the sale of the vehicle, then the insurance company may consider reducing the premium if it obtains sufficient evidence.

Q: How is car insurance affected when a driver, driving under a suspended licence, is charged with causing an accident?

A: Under a no-fault insurance system, an individual would claim from his or her own insurance company. It would then be up to the company to recover any amount paid as a result of the accident. If the other driver drove while under suspension, the insurance company would have further evidence in suing that driver.

Q: An individual whose long-term insurance benefits were cancelled wants them reinstated. How?

A: Long-term insurance coverage is based on medical evidence supporting an individual's claim. The insurance company likely cancelled the coverage because of a medical report indicating that the individual could return to work or was no longer disabled. The alternative at this point is to obtain a further medical opinion with the consent of the company. If this report confirms the disability, then the insurance company will likely reinstate coverage.

Q: Can I sue my insurance company if I have problems collecting disability benefits under my policy?

A: Yes. If the policy clearly entitles you to coverage, and the company refuses to provide an adequate reason for nonpayment, then you have a right to sue the company. If, however, you have received and reviewed an explanation from the company, then a lawsuit is not recommended.

Limiting Liability

When you park your car, you get a slip of paper saying that the attendant is not responsible for damage to your car. When you go to lunch and hang up your coat, you get a slip of paper saying that the restaurant is not responsible for the loss of your coat. When you go to a movie, you get a slip of paper stating that the theatre is not responsible for any injury suffered while you are watching the movie. Some toboggans now carry the following warning:

Wear a helmet at all times. No more than three riders at all times. Do not ride while lying on stomach or back or while standing. Avoid trees, stumps, rocks, branches, or man-made obstacles. Do not use near streets, roadways, driveways, or sidewalks. This product does not have brakes. Do not pull using any motorized or nonmotorized vehicles.

The law is that you cannot get out of liability for negligent conduct even though the slip of paper you get says otherwise. So, if the parking lot attendant does nothing to prevent a group of thugs from entering the lot and smashing your car, the owner will still be held responsible. However, people cannot go around acting carelessly and hoping that the law will protect them. The car left on the lot should be locked. The mink coat should be kept and not checked. Kids should be told that tobogganing is risky. If you have acted responsibly and the other person has not, then and only then will the court compensate you for your loss.

Individual Responsibility

Q: An individual learned that child support payments made to his ex-spouse were keyed into Revenue Canada computers as a moving expense. The two lines appear close to each other on the income tax form. It was a simple error, and no one seemed to be upset. However, Revenue Canada subsequently asked the taxpayer if he had in fact paid child support. What it needed was a receipt from the ex-spouse. This document was eventually supplied to Revenue Canada, which subsequently lost it. The taxpayer went through the process once again. Revenue Canada has now processed the request but refuses to pay any interest since it initially suggested that the original receipt was not sent. Should additional documents be obtained confirming the original receipt?

A: Yes. The more evidence a taxpayer has the better. If the ex-spouse can write a letter, with a copy going to the taxpayer, about past payments, then hopefully Revenue Canada can reconsider his position and pay lost interest. A copy should also be sent to the minister of national revenue so that everyone involved is fully aware that payments were properly sent and that interest should be paid.

Q: An individual was arrested in the United States for possession of an illegal substance. He went to a local jail until the fine was paid and was then released. When he returned by bus to the Canadian border, his impounded car could not be released until an additional fine was paid. He paid part of the fine and returned home without paying the balance. A warrant has been issued for the outstanding fine. He now wishes to reenter the United States but is concerned that he may be arrested. What should he do?

A: The fine should be paid so that there is nothing outstanding on his record. Customs officials should be contacted before travel takes place to ensure that he will not be arrested. This matter should be cleared up sooner rather than later — and not at the border crossing.

Q: One hot summer evening, an individual was sitting on his porch. A neighbour began fighting with her spouse. The noise reached a fevered pitch, and the individual told them to stop. They then began yelling at him, so he "mooned" them. The police were called, and he was charged with indecent exposure. He was convicted. Some years later, he was denied a job because of his criminal record. What can he do?

A: He can obtain a pardon that wipes the slate clean. After the pardon, he can clearly say "No" to the question "Have you ever been convicted of a criminal offence?". A pardon is obtained by filling out forms available at most courthouses and sending them to the solicitor general's office with a small fee. After the paperwork is processed, he will be notified by mail that the pardon has been granted.

Q: At what age can teenagers legally be left alone overnight?

A: At age 12, a mature child can be left alone. If the child is not mature, then he or she cannot be left alone. Legally, you have to be at least 14 years of age to be left by yourself, and in all cases parents are responsible if something goes wrong, until the child reaches the age of majority, which in Ontario is 18.

Steps of a Legal Dispute

1. **Write it down:** Take the time to write out clearly what happened. The process of putting pen to paper will help you to collect your thoughts and give your lawyer the full picture.

2. **Speak to a friend:** Sometimes talking it out with a friend will help you with your choices. Maybe you haven't seen all sides of the problem. Maybe there is an obvious solution to your dilemma.

3. **Write a letter:** If you send a polite letter outlining your concerns, maybe you'll get a proper explanation or even an offer to resolve the dispute.

4. **See a lawyer:** Set up a brief meeting with your lawyer armed with your written story. It will save time, money, and aggravation. The lawyer will tell you if you have a case.

5. **Get a lawyer's letter:** If there is a case, have your lawyer write a letter. It may solve the problem at minimal expense.

6. **Sue:** If all else fails, you may have to sue.

7. **Mediate:** You can now mediate most disputes. Mediation gives you the chance to tell your story in an informal fashion, and it costs less than a lawsuit. You still hire a lawyer, but you can save both time and money by this process.

Health-Care Facilities

Q: How do I get a copy of my medical file?

A: Most hospitals will accept a signed letter requesting a copy of a medical file. A fee will be required as well as either a social insurance number or a date of birth. Medical files are often obtained either to get a second opinion or to launch a lawsuit. As a consumer of medical services, you are entitled to obtain a copy of your file. The one exception is if your treating physician believes that reading the file may cause psychological damage. In that case, he or she has the ultimate discretion to withhold the file.

There is a principle of law called **spoilation**. Under this principle, if a document is intentionally destroyed, then the court can use the fact of destruction (instead of the document) against the person who destroyed it. So, in a recent medical malpractice suit, the destruction of medical records was a factor considered by the court in rendering its decision.

Q: Is in vitro fertilization covered by medicare?

A: The answer depends on where you live and the recommendations of your doctor. In the event that the procedure is not covered, there are appeal options within the medicare system, and eventually the courts can intervene.

Q: How do I evaluate the standard of care that a doctor provides?

A: One way to assess the care provided is to get a second opinion. The current debate in law is whether the standard is that set by the community where the treatment occurred or that set in a larger centre, which may have teaching hospitals or other medical facilities.

Survey

According to the College of Physicians and Surgeons of Ontario, between 1991 and 1995 the number of public complaints against physicians averaged a little over 2,000 per year. Since that time, the number has dropped by half.

Debts

Q: How do I deal with credit card debts?

A: Either directly or through credit-counselling agencies, you can contact the credit card companies and ask for payment plans. Usually, the companies will require financial disclosure, which will show that your debts exceed your ability to pay them. However, over time the debts can be settled. If you have no money, you should consider the option of bankruptcy. Bankruptcy involves hiring a bankruptcy trustee, who is generally an accountant. The trustee will prepare a statement of your assets and liabilities and file it with the court and then ask the court to absolve you from having to pay these debts in order to return to society as a productive individual. The court may impose some restrictions on your bankruptcy, such as requiring you to pay a percentage of your income for a period of time. After that time has expired (generally nine months), your debts are eliminated, and you can attempt to return to a healthy financial state. However, not all debts are cancelled by bankruptcy, such as certain necessities of life (e.g., clothing and food). They will have to be paid for over time, even though your other debts have been cancelled.

Most people apply for credit cards without reading the "fine print." This contract allows credit card companies to seize your bank account and have you pay for 100% of their legal fees if you refuse to pay the debts. Read the fine print.

Q: As a result of bankruptcy, a debt remains unpaid. What recourses, if any, are available?

A: If the debt was incurred prior to the bankruptcy, and the individual received bankruptcy protection, chances are that the debt will be wiped out and that no further recourse will be available. If the debt was incurred after the bankruptcy, however, it is due, just like any other debt.

Bankruptcy

The Bankruptcy and Insolvency Act allows consumers to reorganize their debts and propose plans of payment on a percentage basis over a number of years. For example, if you have debts under $75,000, excluding your mortgage, you can propose to pay your creditors 50 cents on the dollar over five years without liquidating your assets. The new process avoids the need to go to court and places the Revenue authorities with all other creditors.

In the mid-1960s, there were approximately 2,000 bankruptcies per year. By the mid-1990s, this number averaged over 60,000 per year.

Banking

Q: Can a bank withdraw money from an account in order to pay an outstanding loan?

A: Most banks require customers to sign an agreement when a savings or chequing account is opened. This agreement gives the bank the right to withdraw money to pay all outstanding loans. Similarly, most credit cards issued by banks authorize them to withdraw payments from your account if you are delinquent in making your monthly payments.

Q: Am I responsible for legal fees incurred by a bank or trust company when my loan has gone into default?

A: Yes. Most loan agreements or credit card agreements state that you are liable to pay all legal fees incurred by the institution in question. However, if the matter goes to court, all judges retain the discretion to reduce the amount that you are required to pay to the financial institution's lawyer. Costs are governed by the courts, and no agreement can detract from this basic discretion of a judge.

Q: How do I go about enforcing a letter of credit?

A: A letter of credit is akin to a debt that is payable when certain conditions are met. The letter itself may stipulate payment on a set date at a set place. In that case, the letter is usually presented to the financial institution that issued the letter, and payment will be made.

Security for Costs

When you sue someone, he or she can use various tactics to delay the suit. One technique is to ask that the person suing deposit money in the court. This is called **security for costs**. It ensures that if the plaintiff loses he or she can pay for the defendant's legal costs, since the person who wins gets legal costs paid for by the losing side.

The most well-known case involved the widow of Tim Horton and his former business associate Ron Joyce. Mrs. Horton was allowed to sue without depositing money, but she eventually lost her case.

FROM THE ONTARIO COURT OF APPEAL IN THE CASE OF HORTON vs. JOYCE SEPTEMBER 15, 1994

FROM THE JUDGMENT OF FINLAYSON J.:

FINLAYSON J.A. (in Chambers): — This is a motion by the respondents, other than the respondent James W. Blaney, for an order for security for costs under rule 61.06(1)(a) of the Rules of Civil Procedure ("Rules"). I was advised at the opening of this motion that the appeal against Blaney has been abandoned. The rule in question reads as follows:

61.06(1) *In an appeal where it appears that,*

(a) *there is good reason to believe that the appeal is frivolous and vexatious and that the appellant has insufficient assets in Ontario to pay the costs of the appeal;*

. . .

a judge of the appellate court, on motion by the respondent, may make such order for security for costs of the proceeding and of the appeal as is just.

Mrs. Horton, the appellant, is the widow of the late Tim Horton, a professional hockey player of considerable ability, who died in an automobile accident while still in his prime. He and the respondent Joyce had been partners in a franchise operation called "Tim Horton Donuts." On Horton's death, Mrs. Horton inherited her husband's position in the limited partnership which owned the franchise. She and Joyce continued the partnership for a time but the relationship was not a satisfactory one, at least to Joyce, and he suggested that they either buy each other out or both sell to a third party. The result was that Mrs. Horton sold Joyce her shares in the company controlling the franchise for $1 million.

The action which is the subject matter of this appeal arises out of that sale. Mrs. Horton alleges that Joyce took advantage of her inexperience and the fact that she had become dependent upon drugs and amphetamines to induce her to sell her interest in the franchise at an improvident price. Specifically, she pleaded that she did not have the mental capacity to make the financial decision that she did. Her action was against Joyce and the respondent companies for rescission and against her lawyer, Blaney, who advised her at the time, for damages. At the end of a lengthy trial which by agreement was restricted to the threshold issue of liability, the Honourable Madam Justice German reserved judgment. On February 1, 1993, she delivered detailed reasons, numbering 84 pages, dismissing the action with costs. In the course of those reasons, she made findings of credibility adverse to Mrs. Horton and other findings which were supportive of the respondents' witnesses.

. . .

Looking at the material supporting this motion against what I consider to be the overriding qualification of *bona fides*, I do not think that the respondents have made out a case for security for costs. Certainly, Mrs. Horton does not fit into any of the appellant categories set out above. It is conceded that she is a person of limited means, but her complaint is that she was deprived of what was rightfully hers by the conduct of the respondents. She is in no sense a "strawman." She is asserting a cause of action which is hers alone. There is no advantage to her in pursuing the appeal except her belief that she will win it. She has borrowed money to perfect the appeal and her counsel is anxious to obtain a hearing date.

. . .

I think that an early hearing date is desirable, and since both parties seek to expedite the appeal, I am prepared to make such an order. In all other respects, the motion is dismissed. The determination of the costs of the motion is left to the panel hearing the appeal.

Order accordingly.

RRSPs and Pensions

Q: How do I change the beneficiary of an RRSP?

A: An RRSP, like any other investment vehicle, requires you to name a beneficiary. People often designate their estates as the beneficiaries. If you name your estate as the beneficiary, then all money received by your estate will be taxed. If, however, you name an individual as the beneficiary, then money will not be taxed under your estate. If you have named either your estate or an individual and wish to make a change, then all you have to do is approach the financial institution that issued the RRSP and complete a change-of-beneficiary form. It will take effect as soon as it is signed and received by the institution.

An RRSP allows you to accumulate money on a tax-free basis before your retirement. It is limited to age 65.

A RRIF is the savings vehicle used when you reach 71. It requires you to withdraw a set amount every year.

An RESP is a savings vehicle for your children's education. There are no tax deductions available when you contribute to an RESP; however, when the money is withdrawn for your children's education, tax exemptions exist.

Q: What are the pros and cons of an RRSP payable to an estate?

A: If an RRSP is payable to your estate, then it is taxed with all other income under your estate. If it is payable to an individual, then your estate pays no tax on the RRSP.

Q: How do I deal with an RRSP under a will?

A: An RRSP can be specifically mentioned in your will, and it can be made payable to an individual or a charity. If your RRSP is dealt with under your will, then make sure that the RRSP itself has the same beneficiary designated so that there is no conflict between the RRSP and your will.

Q: A Canadian resident working for a Canadian company owned by a U.S. parent experienced difficulties in collecting a pension. What recourses are available?

A: If the Canadian subsidiary is still in business, then it should be contacted in an effort to resolve the dispute. The next step is to contact the head office with proof that the individual was an employee of the Canadian subsidiary. Should both entities refuse to provide coverage, money may have been set aside with provincial licensing authorities (the corporations branch) to cover former Canadian employees. If no money has been set aside, then the only alternative is to sue the American company in a Canadian court in an effort to have the pension paid as a debt to the employee.

Tax Shelters

Every year at tax time, people look for investments that qualify as tax deductions to reduce their tax burdens. There is a wide range of projects called **tax shelters** available, many of which are unregulated.

Traditionally, real estate has formed the most obvious tax shelter. With a minimum down payment, you can arrange with tax shelter promoters for the management of real estate and receive tax write-offs. Inevitably, these investments fail since the promoters of these projects misjudge the income to be derived from the investment. You are then faced not only with a piece of real estate that is not as valuable as anticipated but also with debts associated with the investment.

If you want to invest in these kinds of tax shelters, then make sure that the real estate can support the investment, and get a letter from Revenue Canada confirming that you are allowed to deduct costs associated with the investment. Get audited financial state ments from the promoter, and speak to any lender who advances money on your investment. Be prepared for the investment to collapse, and set aside funds to cover any shortfalls.

Tax Loopholes

Businesses are often creative in the ways that they raise money. In one case, the purchasers of a racetrack found a loophole in RRSP legislation that allowed RRSP money to be invested in race-tracks. All the parties benefited from this creativity. The investors were able to shelter income through an RRSP, and the promoter was able to carry through with the purchase. Loopholes change, and who knows what creativity will occur in the future?

Mutual Funds

Mutual funds are a popular means of saving money for retire-ment. However, as with any other savings vehicle, investors must ask questions and be aware of what they are buying. Remember the basic principle of returns based on risk. In other words, the higher the return, the greater the risk. If an investment pays 20% per year, then it reflects a high level of risk. Contrast that rate with a savings account that earns between three to four per cent. There is little or no risk associated with a savings account.

Remember what a mutual fund sets out to do. You and a group of other people are putting money into a fund, which invests in the stock market. If the stock market decreases, then your fund decreases. Similarly, if your fund sells stock, then doing so may cause a run on the stock market that further depresses not only the market but also the fund in general since you have other investments tied to the market.

A mutual fund is nothing more than a way to invest your money in the stock market. Be prepared for the risk of market decreases.

Copyright

When you buy anything that is packaged, when you read a newspaper, when you write a report on some research that you have done, copyright issues arise. The packaging may be unique and have catchy phrases. The newspaper will have ads and photographs. Your report is the product of your research and thinking. In each case, the owners — designers, publishers, and authors — hold copyright on their intellectual and material work. Copyright protects the owners from others using the work. Stealing someone else's work is an infringement of a right that entitles the owner to sue for the return of the item or its copy and to receive, as payment, any money earned by the work in question.

Q: When can a picture be used for commercial purposes?

A: A person's picture can only be used with his or her permission. This whole issue arose when a woman, sitting on the steps of a public building, was photographed. The picture then appeared on the cover of a local magazine. When she found out, she sued, claiming that her privacy had been invaded by the publication of that picture. The case went to the Supreme Court of Canada, which agreed with her and awarded her compensation.

Q: When a photographer is asked to take a picture of a contest winner, who owns the picture?

A: The contest organizers own the picture. The contest was organized by a certain group, and the public was asked to participate in it. Chances are that the contest rules, the small print at the bottom of an ad or on a contest ticket, stated that the group owned the right to promote the contest winner. The picture is therefore part of the promotion, and the photographer was carrying out the organizers' wishes. If there were no conditions, then the photographer would own the rights to the picture.

Q: Can I copyright pictures of my car or dog?

A: Copyright is the law's way of saying that you invented or own a certain thing. You can copyright the picture in question by registering it formally with the copyrights branch of the federal government or automatically by keeping the negative as proof that you produced that picture. The photo itself is a product of your work and is therefore automatically copyrighted. Since you can't get your pet's consent, the fact that you own the pet determines ownership of the picture.

Q: Are consents required for pictures that appear in high school yearbooks?

A: Since photos and artwork make up a yearbook, the editors should get everyone's consent to use the images in the book.

Q: A piece of art was sent to a friend who took pictures of it and subsequently sold the pictures. Who owns the proceeds received?

A: If the art was sent without permission being given for pictures to be taken, then the original artist owns the pictures and the proceeds from the sale. If permission was given, then the photographer keeps the money.

Q: Can I take a picture of other people's objects, such as a transport truck, a plane, or a train?

A: Nothing stops you from taking the picture; however, if you make money as a result, then you owe money to the owner of that object. For example, if you take a picture of an Air Canada plane, then you would technically owe that airline anything you receive by selling the picture.

Q: A restaurant has been threatened with copyright infringement for using an existing name. What can the owner do?

A: Unfortunately, the owner will have to change the restaurant's name. If you don't have permission to use a name other than your own, then you can't use it. Recently, a well-known U.S. actor had a Canadian restaurant change its name since it was using the actor's name. No employee of the restaurant had a similar name; the owner just liked it.

Q: When does a copyright expire?

A: Copyright exists for the life of the author and expires 50 years after his or her death. After that, you either have to reregister copyright with the federal government or lose the right to use the item exclusively.

A copyright is the right to protect your intellectual work once put on paper.

A patent is the right to protect an object that you have invented.

When you see the words *patent pending*, they mean that papers have been filed with the government but that confirmation of the item's uniqueness and a patent number are still outstanding. The government will verify that the item in question is unique and therefore deserves patent protection. Sometimes patent pending means that the owners of the item intend to get patent protection but don't have the money. They are waiting to see if the product takes off before registering it.

Q: Can I open a store under the name of a popular song?

A: No. The song was written by a person who owns it and the rights to use it. Unless you get his or her permission, you can't use the song. Even if you try using a slight variation, it won't work. In the public's mind, it will be linked to the song, and, as a result, you are capitalizing on someone's work.

Q: Someone has copied my product and made money off it. What can I do?

A: You'll have to sue the individual to recover the money. In order to prevent the product's sale to someone else, you may consider contacting the likely buyers and warning them that a certain person may try to sell them a product that you own. If you have proof of ownership, then you would not be damaging the other person's reputation, and you are entitled to protect your interests.

**FROM THE FEDERAL COURT
IN THE CASE OF APPLE vs. MACINTOSH
APRIL 29, 1986**

FROM THE JUDGMENT OF MR. JUSTICE REED:

REED J.: — The issue for decision in this case is a narrow but important one: is a computer program when embodied in a silicon chip in the computer a subject-matter in which copyright exists? Many of the facts are not greatly in dispute. The plaintiff holds a registered copyright in two computer programs: Autostart ROM, registration No. 319,465, October 8, 1982, and Applesoft, registration No. 319,468, October 8, 1982.

. . .

The two programs in question were created for the purpose of being encoded on chips (silicon semi-conductors) to be mounted in the plaintiffs' Apple II+ computer, to serve as the operating instructions for that computer. While only eight lines of one of the programs have been reproduced above, each of the programs in issue contains more than a thousand such lines of instruction.

There is no doubt that the creation of a computer program requires a great deal of time, effort, and ingenuity. Professor Graham, an acknowledged expert in computer programming, gave evidence that it would take four months for him, with the help of two students, to write programs to serve the same purpose as those in issue in this case.

There is no doubt that computer programs are highly individualistic in nature and contain a form of expression personal to the individual programmer. No two programmers would ever write a program in exactly the same way (except perhaps in the case of the most simple program). Even the same programmer, after writing a program and leaving it for some time, would not write the program the same way on a second occasion. The sequence of instructions would most certainly be different. The possibility of two programmers creating identical programs, without copying, was compared by the defendants' expert witness to the likelihood of a monkey sitting at a typewriter producing Shakespeare.

TV Images

A photographer takes a picture of you as part of a crowd or walking down the street, and that picture later appears in a newspaper or on TV. You and your family think it is great that your picture is seen by others. But what if that picture is sold and

used in some TV or magazine advertisement or is repeated in newscasts? Have your rights been breached?

In 1998, the Supreme Court of Canada awarded a woman $2,000 because her picture was taken without her permission. When is the line drawn between freedom of the press to report and the privacy of an individual? If you are part of a demonstration and there is a public interest to show the crowd, the media do not need to obtain each person's consent and pay each person a fee. Similarly, if you are a public figure, your picture can be used over and over. However, if you are approached on the street for a comment, the interviewer must ask for your consent and permission to use your image and whatever you say in subsequent broadcasts.

Y2K

The Y2K problem arose when computers read the year 2000 as the year 1900. Older computers were programmed to read only the last two digits of the year. The problem affected computer programs that are date sensitive, such as programs that calculate interest based on a date. For example, if you owed interest from October 1999 to February 2000, a computer may have calculated interest from 1900 to 1999. Y2K did not affect most mechanical devices that do not depend on the date in order to function. What were the legal implications when something went wrong?

First, there was the cost incurred in making computer systems ready for the year 2000 and beyond. Consumers resisted attempts by companies to pass these costs on to goods and services. Companies and individuals have made claims against hardware and software manufacturers to recover these costs.

Second, there was the liability of company directors. If they did not take steps to ensure that their company was Y2K compliant, they faced personal liability for any damages to the company and its shareholders. Companies are required to report to the various securities commissions. Some companies may have argued that they couldn't report financial data due to Y2K problems. Some may have said that their data were subject to revision. Accurate financial reporting is a serious concern to investors since commissions can impose fines. Directors and officers may be sued for any losses that result. The damages would be the difference between the financial results achieved and the financial results that would have been achieved but for the Y2K problem.

Third, if something went wrong, people tried to claim compensation under their insurance policies. Many insurance companies denied that they were liable, arguing that their insurance contracts did not offer this type of coverage. Individuals argued that the insurance was meant to cover all manner of loss and that this type of loss was not specifically excluded. Nonetheless, many insurance companies wrote to their customers stating that Y2K problems were not covered by existing policies.

In the United States, laws were passed to limit Y2K liability in the event of a lawsuit. No such limits exist in Canada. Regardless of your right to sue, make sure that you retain paper records to verify the information received from companies such as banks and brokerage houses.

Q: My computer is 10 years old and has failed. Can I sue?

A: There are two basic limits on your right to sue. First, you are limited to claims that are six years old or less. This is called a **limitation period**. Second, you have to try to fix the problem on your own. This is called **mitigation**. In this case, you can't sue given the age of your computer.

Q: What are the limits on my right to sue in the United States?

A: U.S. law limits **punitive damages** (i.e., a penalty award or fine) at three times your loss or $250,000, whichever is less. This limit applies to individuals whose net worth is $500,000 or less and to businesses with fewer than 50 employees. Your loss itself is also restricted unless you were intentionally targeted by the person sued.

Q: How would insurance cover my computer problems?

A: Most homeowner's policies provide for insurance coverage when your property is damaged by fire or "other events." If your computer has ceased operating due to internal problems associated with Y2K, this may qualify as "other events." Read your policy, see if there is coverage, and contact your insurance broker to discuss this type of loss.

Q: How are company directors liable?

A: Company directors are liable for certain company-related events. For example, they are liable for unpaid wages and may be liable for poor financial results. Directors often resign when a company has lost money. In a similar fashion, if a director failed to take steps or have senior management take steps to protect the company from Y2K problems, he or she may have been forced to resign or may have been liable if reckless in managing the company. If directors were warned but took no steps, they may have been liable.

Q: I bought a program said to be Y2K compliant, but it didn't work. What can I do?

A: It's no different than buying a toaster that doesn't work. You bought a defective product that can be returned for cash or a replacement.

Q: A travel brochure indicated that the tour operator would not be liable for any loss suffered as a result of the Y2K problem. What were the implications of this statement?

A: By warning customers before they travelled, the tour operator was telling them that there were risks involved. If something went wrong, the operator could then point to the brochure and deny any liability. It was "buyer beware." If there was no warning, the operator would have been liable, as with any other mishap that may have occurred as a result of his or her mistakes.

Q: Were there any limits on what was a Y2K problem?

A: The loss that you suffered must have been directly related to the Y2K issue. If a bank machine didn't work because of vandalism, Y2K couldn't have been blamed for the problem. It must have been directly caused by computers going awry because of the date change.

Q: Are there options available besides suing in court?

A: Yes. Many companies have announced a system of informal arbitration to settle claims on a quick and cost-efficient basis. Arbitration avoids the necessity of going to court.

Q: Have there been any successful lawsuits?

A: Since the Y2K problem is new and you have up to six years to sue, the dust has yet to settle on this question. As with any lawsuit, you have to suffer a loss, and only when your loss has not been covered or fixed would you consider going to court. To date, only one known lawsuit has been started in Canada.

Q: There were reports that some software used for Internet credit card purchases was not Y2K compliant. Who was liable in this case?

A: There is special software used for credit card purchases over the Internet called encryption software. Some of these programs expired in 2000. Yet, because there were warnings, and because using a credit card over the Internet is like using it over the phone, it became "buyer beware." Credit card information should only be given to known companies and suppliers.

Q: Should I have been worried about Y2K?

A: No. In part, the threat of legal proceedings caused many companies to anticipate problems and plan for year 2000 and beyond. From a business point of view, it was in a company's best interest to continue building consumer confidence. You needn't have worried.

CHAPTER THREE

Employment Rights

Fired for cause means that an employer has a valid reason to fire an employee and tells that employee why he or she is no longer required by the company. **Constructive dismissal** means that you no longer have a job but that no one has told you why you were fired.

There are several ways to lose a job. One can be fired for cause, meaning that some major error has occurred. One can also quit or voluntarily resign. A situation that often leads to lawsuits is when one is fired without apparent reason. This is called **wrongful dismissal**.

The first step is to try to obtain an explanation from your employer. It may be that an overall downsizing has occurred and that, through some administrative error, you were not given a proper explanation. If, however, you have asked and no explanation has been given, then as a former employee you are entitled to find out why you are no longer employed by that company. You may have to consider launching a lawsuit to obtain not only an explanation but also a severance package that may be due to you.

A severance package is often governed by provincial laws, which set out the minimum severance that has to be paid depending on your years of service. If you have not been given an explanation but have received severance pay, then the purpose of the lawsuit is to obtain an explanation or better severance if you haven't released your rights. An explanation may also be provided in the form of employment insurance documentation that an employer is required to send to you at the end of your employment. The various employment codes on this form may provide you with an explanation.

If you have not received any severance forms, then the first step is not to sue but to contact Human Resources Development Canada, the government agency that takes care of employment matters.

Regardless of the reason for your dismissal, you may consider requesting a letter of reference so that you can apply for other jobs. If you have been fired for cause, however, it is unlikely that you will receive such a letter.

Employees and employers are often governed by employment contracts, which imply that employer and employee have signed a formal document that sets out each party's respective rights and obligations both during employment and after termination. These agreements will specify the amount of severance that you are to receive and will spell out when an employer can dismiss an employee.

Employers often provide employees with counselling or placement services. These services give employees chances to prepare résumés and market their services. This is part of a trend that employers must follow for mid- to high-level employees to ensure that the transition to a new job is as smooth as possible.

People take a lot of pride in their work since it often defines the individual. It is not surprising, therefore, that employment problems arise on a daily basis. The problem may be as small as a dispute with a coworker or being upset about not getting a big enough raise. It may be serious enough that you quit.

The Supreme Court of Canada recently reviewed the area of

wrongful dismissal and laid down some basic rules.

1. Courts will not condone insensitive treatment when people are fired. For example, a boss cannot yell at you across the office floor and say "You're fired!"
2. Given the importance that we all place on work and income, an employee is most vulnerable at the time of being let go. Courts will determine if employers acted properly at the time of dismissal and will intervene to protect the rights of employees who are vulnerable.
3. Employers should be candid, reasonable, and honest with their employees. Humiliation and embarrassment will not be condoned. For example, an employer should clearly tell the employee that he or she is no longer required at the place of work due to past errors. An employer cannot say "You no longer have a job" without saying why.

In the pages that follow, we will explore as many employment situations as possible, and as always the best advice is to take time to settle down and then, in a calm manner, speak to your boss. Maybe it was an oversight. Maybe it was a problem that wasn't communicated to you. In any event, try not to rush out and sue your boss. Talk it out.

Cause

Q: What are my rights if I am let go without cause?

A: "Cause" means that an employer has a valid reason to fire an employee. If the reason is valid, then there is little that can be done other than ensuring that proper termination papers are issued and accumulated vacation pay is paid. If there is no valid cause, then a severance package is due based on the years of service and the position held in the company.

Q: After completing part-time employment, an employee was offered full-time employment. With the full-time position came a period of probation. During the probationary period, the person was fired. What remedies are available?

A: If the probationary period was explained, then the employer can terminate employment if doing so was not planned. If the probationary period was not explained, then the employer must have a valid reason for firing the worker.

Q: What is the benchmark for compensation after three years of employment?

A: The rule of thumb is one month for every year of service. Although this rule has been criticized, it is often the guide used by employers and some courts.

If an employer changes the fundamental terms of employment without saying "You're fired," then you have been wrongfully dismissed. The legal term is "constructive dismissal." In other words, no one has said that you no longer have a job, but the fundamental nature of the job has changed, and you can consider yourself fired.

So, if an employer says that you no longer work nine to five but nine to nine, then that is a major change. If you had 10 subordinates and now you have only one, then you have been fired. This is of course subject to the employer's giving you a valid explanation for the change. It may be based on a corporate reorganization that is fully justified. However, if you are the only one in a whole organization who has been affected, then clearly the writing is on the wall.

Q: An employee has not been dismissed but believes that she will be in 30 days. What should she do to be prepared?

A: When an employee is told that she is being fired, she should be polite and ask for an explanation. If there is a valid explanation, then there is nothing she can do. She should not argue if the reason is trumped up. She should leave the workplace as soon as possible in order to collect her thoughts and determine her next course of action. She may consider writing a letter disputing the termination or seeking adequate compensation. If a fair package is not offered, then a lawyer's letter may assist in resolving the dispute.

Money

Q: After 18 years of service, a writer was fired without any explanation and with a record of positive performance. He was offered a package just short of what he was entitled to receive. Why do employers offer reduced severance packages?

A: Employers know what they have to pay when they fire employees. They have access to legal advice. However, they also know that there is a cost for an employee who takes them to court, because the employee has to hire a lawyer. They often factor in this cost and reduce the severance amount accordingly. For example, if an employee is entitled to $10,000 but would have to pay $2,000 in legal fees, he or she would net approximately $8,000 in court. An employer may therefore offer $9,000, knowing that the employee would not spend money on a lawyer in order to get the difference. It often becomes a question of economics, not the right of an employee to receive full compensation.

Q: An employee was dismissed for not reaching certain sales targets. The company clearly stated to him that the targets were unrealistic given its geographical area and historical performance. On dismissal, he was offered slightly more than the minimum required by law. Is this fair?

A: The company obviously realized that its targets were unreasonable and decided to reorganize operations. In offering more than the minimum, it implicitly recognized that things did not work out, and the employee was compensated as a result. Unless he was lured away from another job and there are witnesses to the unrealistic targets, there is little that can be done. If, however, there is additional documentation, then he may be entitled to receive a slightly better severance package. Ultimately, though, when an employee is terminated, all that an employer or court can do is increase the level of compensation.

Q: An employee was fired on December 24, at the end of the day, for using company paper for personal use. She was innocent and wanted to know her rights.

A: Employment specialists always advise employers never to fire people on Christmas Eve since it is emotionally hard on employees. The employee should be given the chance to explain; otherwise, she can sue for damages suffered.

Q: An individual was laid off and offered a severance package. After considering the package, he signed a release. He has come to realize that he should have obtained a slightly better package. What can he do?

A: When you take the time to consider a package offered to you and then sign a release, there is little that you can do to alter the settlement with your ex-employer. Releases usually contain provisions that the individual can read and understand English and sign the release after considering the amount offered. In this case, because the employee took the time to consider the offer before signing the release, there is little that he can do to reopen the settlement.

Noncompetition

Q: On employment termination, a noncompetition agreement is required. Does the employee have to sign the agreement?

A: If the type of work is confidential, then the employer can insist on such an agreement being signed. The agreement must be reasonable in terms of time and area of work covered. If it was never contemplated between the parties, then the employee can refuse to sign it.

Q: An individual set up shop across the street from his old employer and is now directly competing using information learned from the old workplace. Can the ex-employer do anything?

A: If the individual has clearly taken information from the ex-employer and used it to compete, then the old employer can sue the individual to prevent this activity from continuing. It becomes a question of whether the business methods are unique and therefore owned by the old employer. If that is the case, then the new business can be closed down, or the ex-employee may have to pay the ex-employer compensation for using its techniques.

Although you can prevent an ex-employee from competing against you, you cannot prevent an ex-employee from ever working again.

Noncompetition agreements must be reasonable in terms of the length of time that an ex-employee cannot compete and the geographical area in which he or she cannot set up shop. If either condition is breached, then the noncompetition clause can be struck out.

Q: An employee for a major wine retailer was told that she could never work for the organization because she would be in a conflict of interest. Can an employer prevent an employee from working for another company or organization?

A: Unless there is a noncompetition clause in a contract or a signed paper saying that the employee cannot compete with the company by taking another job, nothing can stop her from working for any other organization. No one can interfere with her ability to work without paying her adequate compensation. If an employee changes jobs, it is incumbent on her to tell her new employer that she has had access to information that she must keep confidential. The new employer will surely understand and not try to force that information out of the new employee. This may give the old employer some comfort, but the old employer cannot prevent the employee from working elsewhere.

Q: Some nonprofit agencies require their employees to attend annual meetings without pay. Some employers have this as a specific clause in their employment agreements. Is this enforceable?

A: If the employment contract requires attendance at certain meetings, and the contract has been voluntarily signed, then the requirement is clearly enforceable. It is not an unreasonable part of the job. However, if the expectations placed on an employee are unreasonable, then they are unenforceable.

Q: A midlevel manager responded to an ad for a contractual/term placement of one year outside Canada. After the usual interviews, he was offered a position that involved a base salary and a housing allowance. He was told that he would be able to find housing at a certain price and that groceries would not exceed a certain amount. On the basis of these promises and the salary offered, he accepted the job. When he showed up for work, the local manager advised him that his hours were not as discussed in Canada and that the cost of living was not as set out. The local boss indicated that it was a take-it or leave-it situation. The manager resigned and returned to Canada but has been unable to return to his previous employment. What can he do?

A: The manager was duped into leaving his previous employment. He accepted the offer of employment, thus forming a contract that the new employer did not respect. This breach entitles the manager to compensation for lost income and inconvenience. He should set out his claim in a letter to the employer; should compensation not be offered, he has no alternative but to sue for all his losses.

Q: An employee worked in outdoor nonurban areas doing manual labour. The foreman of the work crew had a cell phone. The employee used the cell phone to make a personal call to arrange for that evening's accommodation. He wished to stay with a friend and not in the hotel room paid for by the company. He was fired on the spot for unauthorized use of company property, even though he offered to pay for the cost of the phone call. Because he was fired for supposedly ignoring company rules, government insurance benefits are unavailable. What can the employee do?

A: If the employee is governed by a contract or collective agreement that prohibits personal phone calls, then there is little that he can do. If there is nothing prohibiting use of the company phone, then the firing was just an excuse. Ultimately, the company would have saved the cost of a hotel room, and it appears that the employee was treated arbitrarily. He is entitled to sue not only for lost income but also for loss of employment benefits that would be due if he were laid off or if the work term was completed.

Downsizing

Q: An employee was downsized and offered a partial pension windup in what was called an "actuarially reduced pension." What does this mean?

A: When an employee is downsized, the employer often transfers accumulated pension benefits to the employee through an RRSP. Since pension contributions are made toward a future retirement, the employer often counts on interest accumulating to make up the full amount of pension due on retirement. Because the pension plan is being wound up, the employer offers a reduced amount based on what the pension is worth today and not on what it will be worth on retirement. This is called an **actuarially reduced pension**. Simply put, it is the pension in today's dollars versus future dollars. To properly determine whether this is an accurate amount, an employee should consult his or her accountant to check if the calculations were done properly.

Q: Through downsizing, a government agency is being privatized, and the employees are all being laid off. A union is attempting to negotiate a fair severance package. What can the employees do to clarify their rights?

A: When an agency is downsized, the government often provides a set level of severance for the employees. A private company often rehires the employees, or the government pays a proper severance. If neither entity offers a severance package, then the employees are entitled to a claim for lost wages. The best scenario is to have the union negotiate a fair compensation package for all its members.

Working for a member of Parliament has its perks. You can work in one of the most prestigious buildings in Canada and have access to Canadian lawmakers. You get to see how laws are created and eventually passed. However, the downside is that some employees are treated as serfs, required to work long hours with little compensation for overtime. MPs often argue that their employees' salary scales are slightly higher than those in the private sector in order to compensate for this inequity. However, MPs are no different from any other Canadian employer and are required to respect the laws of the land. In some recent well-publicized cases, certain MPs believed that they could fire employees on maternity leave. Legislation exists that protects employees when they take maternity leave, and the MPs were required to give them back their jobs or adequately compensate them for the firing. It took over two years of litigation to reaffirm this principle.

Q: A government employee voluntarily agreed to change full-time employment to a year-to-year contract. This contract was renewed on three occasions but not on the fourth. Under the contract, no severance is due at the end of the term. What can be done?

A: The conditions of employment are set out in the contract. It is a year-to-year contract that is not automatically renewed and has been properly cancelled at the end of that term, so no severance package is due. Unless the contract provides otherwise, being a term employee is no different than cutting someone's lawn on a one-time basis. Once you have completed cutting the lawn, the work is at an end, and nothing other than what is set out in the contract is due. The best alternative is to negotiate a severance package in the contract should it not be renewed at the end of the set term.

Q: An employee in a downsizing situation was offered a severance package that would be reduced if she found other employment. Is this proper?

A: When an employer offers a severance package, it must be based on years of service, and it cannot be reduced if the employee obtains another job. The rule of reducing compensation applies only when an employee has been dismissed and has taken the matter to court. If you sue for 10 months of salary after dismissal but were employed for five of those months, then five months will be deducted based on a principle called **mitigation**. However, that rule does not apply in downsizing.

Q: A middle-level manager with employees reporting to him was informed that the company was closing his division. He would remain in his job, but it would be materially changed. What are his rights?

A: It appears that the employee has not been terminated but no longer has any responsibilities. Although this is not a clear-cut case of termination, if there is no work associated with the job, then it can be considered constructive dismissal: the job has been fundamentally changed, and that change amounts to being fired. The manager should meet with his bosses and negotiate either a new position within the company or a proper severance package.

How to Fire

Although there is never a good time to fire an employee, or to be dismissed as an employee, there are some practical rules that should be followed.

1. Never fire an employee on a Friday; he or she will spend the weekend stewing about what happened and will be unable to contact any prospective employers since most offices work on a Monday-to-Friday basis.

2. Never fire an employee just before a holiday. It is the same as firing a worker on a Friday.

3. Never fire a employee about to go on vacation or a business trip. There is nothing worse than firing an employee about to enter a business meeting in another town.

4. Never fire an employee in public; the embarrassment caused will increase the employer's monetary liability to the employee.

5. Always have a witness present who can testify as to what happened.

There is an urban legend involving a lawyer who fired his assistant. He told his assistant that she would no longer be working for him. She stated that if the boss was serious she would rip her dress and yell "Rape!". The boss, who smoked cigars and was smoking at the time, said "Okay, you're fired." She proceeded to rip her dress and yell "Rape!". The police arrived. The first thing the boss said to the police officer was "Look at the cigar in my right hand. You will note that the ash on the tip of my cigar is several inches long. If you time how long it takes for the cigar to burn that amount, and given that it is still in my hand, there is no way that I could have raped my assistant. There are witnesses present who can testify as to when she entered my office." Charges were laid against the assistant for nuisance and causing a disturbance, and no charge of rape was laid against the boss.

**FROM THE SUPREME COURT OF CANADA
IN THE CASE OF WALLACE vs. UNITED GRAIN
OCTOBER 30, 1997**

FROM THE JUDGMENT OF MR. JUSTICE IACOBUCCI:

Thus, for most people, work is one of the defining features of their lives. Accordingly, any change in a person's employment status is bound to have far-reaching repercussions. In "Aggravated Damages and the Employment Contract", *supra*, Schai noted at p. 346 that, "[w]hen this change is involuntary, the extent of our 'personal dislocation' is even greater."

The point at which the employment relationship ruptures is the time when the employee is most vulnerable and hence, most in need of protection. In recognition of this need, the law ought to encourage conduct that minimizes the damage and dislocation (both economic and personal) that result from dismissal. In *Machtinger, supra*, it was noted that the manner in which employment can be terminated is equally important to an individual's identity as the work itself (at p. 1002). By way of expanding upon this statement, I note that the loss of one's job is always a traumatic event. However, when termination is accompanied by acts of bad faith in the manner of discharge, the results can be especially devastating. In my opinion, to ensure that employees receive adequate protection, employers ought to be held to an obligation of good faith and fair dealing in the manner of dismissal, the breach of which will be compensated for by adding to the length of the notice period.

Retirement

Q: Most employees are required to retire at age 65. During the course of employment, an individual will have paid into the employment insurance fund and will not be able to collect any of those benefits. Can an employee recover amounts paid to the fund on retirement?

A: Laws are enacted for the benefit of the general population. Given that the vast majority of working individuals are under the age of 65, they are well served by the employment insurance scheme. Unfortunately, the plans as they exist discriminate against older employees, and such discrimination will become a larger factor as the population ages. As more people reach mandatory retirement age, and fewer people are in younger age groups, discrimination rules will kick in. Government policies and plans will change as the population ages. For now, however, there is no challenge possible to employment insurance benefits as they exist.

Q: An individual was laid off when she reached the age of 65. Are there any recourses?

A: If there are other employees at the company who are over the age of 65, then the layoff is clearly discriminatory. If it is company policy to lay off all employees at age 65, then the only alternative is to ensure that there is an adequate pension or severance payment made.

Changes at Work

Q: A job advertised as requiring 40 hours a week now requires an additional 10 to 20 hours a week of unpaid time. Can an employer force an employee to work these additional hours?

A: If there is no written contract, then the advertisement is considered an invitation to enter into a contract. When the employee accepts the position, an implied contract is formed based on the terms of the advertisement. An employer cannot force an employee to work an additional 10 to 20 hours per week. If the employer tries to do so, then it may be considered wrongful dismissal. When an employer changes the fundamental terms of the employment, the employee can consider this action a dismissal.

More and more companies are moving from a straight employment relationship to one based on a written contract. Employees are required to sign this contract at the beginning of the work term. This ensures that the terms and conditions of the employment are clearly set out, and, in the event of the employee being fired, severance is clearly spelled out and agreed to by both the employer and the employee.

Q: A long-term employee was told that she would now become an independent contractor and that she would no longer continue as a regular employee. If she refused to accept this change, then she would be laid off. Is this cause for dismissal?

A: An employer cannot change the terms of employment without the employee's agreement. In this case, the employer must have a reason for changing the terms of employment from that of a simple employer-employee relationship to that of an independent-contractor relationship. If there are no justifiable reasons for this change, then it can be considered a dismissal. The employee would be entitled to sue and claim, in general, for a maximum of one month for every year of service.

Maternity Leave

Q: An employee went on maternity leave and received employment insurance benefits. The Employment Insurance Department (HRDC) is now claiming that she received too much money since she is registered as a co-owner of her husband's business. At no time did she receive money from the business. Can Employment Insurance take back the money paid?

A: There is a procedure within the Employment Insurance Department to test decisions made by bureaucrats. In this case, if it can be shown that no benefits were received by the person taking parental leave, then the decision will likely be reversed, and no refund will be required. The rules require that all income be taken into account; if no money was received, then no deductions should be made.

Q: A single parent worked for a company and took courses to improve her qualifications. When other jobs opened up in the company, she was denied a promotion in favour of childless individuals. She subsequently resigned given the workplace environment. Are there any recourses?

A: Although her resignation was voluntary, the facts amount to discrimination, and she can consider herself dismissed because she was denied advancement based on her personal situation. An employer cannot discriminate against employees on the basis of gender or family situation. Her resignation occurred because of an intolerable work environment, and she is entitled to compensation. However, before she initiates a lawsuit, she should clearly write out the events that occurred and forward them to a senior officer at the company, seeking either reinstatement or adequate compensation.

Q: An employee is working part time after returning from maternity leave. There are no set hours as long as the work is completed. An issue has arisen as to whether or not she qualifies for paid statutory holidays. (Statutory holidays are available to all employees, and they are able to take days off, such as Christmas Day and New Year's Day, with pay.) The employer has suggested that since she does not work a regular shift, say from nine to five, statutory holiday pay is not due. She has suggested that applicable legislation does not set out the daily hours of work. They are unable to agree on how to resolve this issue. What can be done?

A: If prior to taking maternity leave the employee received pay for statutory holidays, then this arrangement should continue on her return to work. An employer cannot change the terms of employment when an employee comes back from maternity leave. On her return to work, the company is required to give her her old job with the same terms and conditions that existed before maternity leave. These terms include all benefits and statutory holidays. Unfortunately, the parties have been unable to solve the problem, and, short of taking the matter to court, it may be wise to find a third party to mediate the dispute and settle the issue once and for all.

> **Q:** A three-year employee was recently promoted. She was informed at that time that she would be given regular appraisals and receive a pay raise if her work was satisfactory. Six months into the new position, a review took place, and she received a recommendation for a raise. Upper management refused to grant the raise since they found out that she would be going on maternity leave. What is the employer's responsibility?
>
> **A:** An employer cannot discriminate on the basis that an employee is pregnant. She can either complain to the Human Rights Commission or the Ministry of Labour or take the matter to court. If, while she is pursuing these remedies, the company decides to terminate her position, then it is further liable for damages since it must keep the job open until the issue of discrimination is resolved. It is always difficult for employees to enforce their rights, because management may make daily life difficult.

Disclosure

Q: An employee went on disability for psychological reasons. He has now applied for another job in another company, and the question is whether the old employer is required to disclose the reasons for disability to a new employer.

A: If the new employer has asked for a reference and an explanation as to why the employee was not working, then the old employer is required to disclose all relevant information. Failure to disclose this information may cause the new employer to sue the old employer for false statements or for withholding material facts. The issue of confidentiality, however, must also be considered. If, for example, the psychological disability was important to the job, then it must be disclosed. If it had no bearing on the employee's performance, then it can be withheld. There is a fine line between disclosing personal information and being honest and straightforward with new employers.

Q: Some sports organizations hire employees on a part-time basis for a set period of time depending on the sport in question. Ski coaches, for example, often work during the winter but not in the summer. These employees are not contract but seasonal employees. Their terms are renewed at the beginning of the sport's season. In one case, the organization did not wish to invite a coach back for the next season. Is there an obligation to rehire the coach?

A: If there is an expectation to be rehired on a year-to-year basis, then at the end of the seasonal work the employee should be told that this is his or her last season. If there is no expectation to be rehired on a year-to-year basis, then the employee should be advised that no work is being offered for the sport's upcoming season. Much depends on the organization. Some professionals, such as teachers, work from September to June but are paid an annual salary. If the sports organization pays salaries on a yearly basis, then the employee is not truly a seasonal employee and is working on a year-to-year basis. In that situation, proper notice has to be given as soon as the organization has made a decision not to rehire the employee. It is always best to have the terms of the agreement set out in writing.

A **letter of offer** is a letter sent from an employer to a future employee outlining the terms and conditions of employment. If accepted, it acts as a contract between the two parties. If the company refuses to follow the terms of the letter, the employee has a claim for breach of contract and can sue the company. It is always best to work things out between the company and the employee prior to any lawsuit being initiated.

Students

Q: A 16-year-old student worked in a body shop and was paid by the hour. The employer fell behind in payments, and when the student claimed money owed the employer said that past work was not satisfactory and that money would be deducted from his pay. Does the employee have any recourse?

A: There is no automatic right to set off money owed to the employer from money owed to the employee. In this case, if the student has witnesses that the work was properly performed, then the money is due. Perhaps the employer is just using this as an excuse to pay less money. If the employer has suffered losses, however, then the proper course is to pay the employee the money and have him acknowledge a debt and enter into a repayment plan.

Q: As part of a community college employment program, a student worked part time in a local business. The college paid a grant to the business. Things proceeded smoothly until the owner asked the student if she wouldn't mind waiting for her paycheque since cash flow was tight and he needed the money to pay certain bills. If she insisted on getting her pay, then the company would go bankrupt, and no one would get anything. She agreed, and this situation continued for several months. Thereafter, she occasionally received a salary on an irregular basis. She eventually quit since she was owed thousands of dollars. She then began asking the employer on a regular basis when she would be paid, and occasionally she received small amounts of money, far short of what she was owed. The company eventually filed for bankruptcy, and there are no assets to pay the student. What can she do?

A: It seems that the company used the student's salary to run the business. It had obtained a grant from the community college for a part-time employment program and obviously used the money for business rather than her salary. This is close to fraud or breach of trust in that money was given for a specific purpose: paying the student. Since there is no money in the bankruptcy, the only alternative is for the college or the police to investigate the owner and charge him with fraud or breach of trust if there is sufficient evidence. The student can sue him, but there is no money to pay her even if she is successful. Directors of companies, however, are responsible for unpaid wages, and if the individual owner has assets they will ultimately be seized and sold to pay for the student's salary. Her best alternative, therefore, is to sue the owner for the unpaid wages. This experience has certainly been a lesson to the student on the pitfalls of the workplace.

Injuries

Q: An employee was injured on the work site, received treatment, and returned to work. Some time after his return to work, the injuries reappeared, leading to more time off work. When he was able to return to work, the company refused to reintegrate him but offered a retraining course. He was unable to complete the course due to the injuries. Since he did not complete the retraining, insurance benefits were stopped. What can he do?

A: The common factor in these events is the injury that occurred on the work site. Both the employer and the insurance company should be advised that the events all relate to one injury that occurred on the job site. The employee should be covered by insurance benefits whether or not he completed the retraining. This is a classic case in which he could not complete his job function (work or retraining) and should be entitled to receive long-term disability benefits. The best course of action is to obtain up-to-date medical advice and forward it to both the employer and the insurance company.

Small Businesses

Q: Two friends started a company, with one of the friends putting up his money and the other putting up his skills. Each was to receive a share of the company. They never generated documentation, however; since the company was growing, and the two friends were working full time, their concerns centred on establishing the business. As it progressed, they needed more money to fund operations, and one of the partners had a family member inject money into the company. Eventually, it failed, with no documentation showing each partner's interest or the family member who had lent money to the company. Trade creditors are demanding money, and the partners are not speaking to each other. What can be done?

A: Without anything in writing, they will have a hard time proving who owes what to whom. There may be a moral obligation to repay the family member who invested money, but there is little else that can be done between the partners. However, if one of the partners pays trade creditors, then he would have a claim against the other partner for an equal contribution. The parties should sit down and hammer out an agreement about the responsibility for company debts, salaries, and family investments. If no agreement can be reached, then a lawsuit is the only choice if each partner can prove what happened by means of independent witnesses. One partner's word against the other may not be enough. The moral of the story is that, regardless of how close a friend you have, it is always wise to put down the terms of your agreement in writing.

Suing Your Family

Someone once said that you should never discuss religion or politics at a family dinner. I would add that you should stay away from doing business with family members unless you are absolutely sure that you know what you are doing and put everything in writing.

A client once came to me asking whether he could sue his father. Apparently, the son opened a business, and the father provided some financing. The business failed, but just before it closed its doors the father went in, took some of the store's contents, and changed the locks. The son was therefore denied access to his business and whatever money was left. He was also left with liabilities to the landlord and certain trade creditors. The father, who frankly had the right to take certain items since he had provided the money for the business, would not speak to the son. The son was obviously angry at the father and wanted to sue him. Neither had anything in writing, and after much thought and debate a lawsuit was started, and judgment was granted in favour of the son. The father declared bankruptcy shortly thereafter, so the son was left holding all the debts without any compensation.

I have since lost touch with the client, and I am not sure whether he now speaks to his father. Law may provide an alternative, but it is always best to put things in writing or avoid doing business with members of your family.

Q: A small company was set up by a husband and a wife. They were the only shareholders and directors. One of their employees was injured on the job site and filed a worker's compensation claim. The Worker's Compensation Board — in Ontario now called the Workplace Safety and Insurance Board (WSIB) — investigated the claim and ultimately denied any insurance coverage. The employee believed that she was still unable to work and refused to return to the job site. She wrote a letter asking the employer for compensation since she had worked for many years and was not returning to work. (Under Worker's Compensation Board rules, the job must be kept open for the employee

to return to work after the illness or injury has passed.) She is considering challenging the Worker's Compensation Board, and if she is successful she is entitled to benefits and a job at the end of her benefit period. The employer has also found out that she works part time in another job with another company. What can the employer do?

A: Although the employer must keep a job open, if the employee shows signs of not returning to work, then the employer can clearly argue that she has quit. She has refused to go back to work and is working elsewhere. The employer should write a letter to her clearly stating that the job was offered but declined and that the employee has chosen to seek other employment, implying that she is not interested in returning to her old job. If she is successful in claiming worker's compensation, when that benefit period ends it is unlikely that she will return to her old job. It is important to sort out in writing what happened and send it to the employee so that there is no dispute down the road as to what happened and when.

Corporate directors are liable not only for unpaid wages but also for certain unpaid taxes. Directors often resign prior to the demise of a company in order to avoid this future liability.

Unions

Q: A unionized employee insists that the company establish proper financial audits and a system of checks and balances to ensure that it is financially viable. Not all union members agree with his approach. Some believe that the employee should just do his job, whereas others agree that their jobs would be more secure if the company were on a sounder financial footing. The employee is in a precarious position not only with the employer, who may decide to fire him, but also with the union, which may not come to his aid. What can he do?

A: If the concerns of the unionized employee are legitimate and aimed at ensuring that the company is on a sound financial footing, then his actions are clearly justified. It appears that the problems are internal to the union. If it is affiliated with a larger organization, then that organization should be contacted and the problem explored. If the larger organization refuses to get involved, then the ultimate option is to go to court to place the union under **trusteeship**. Under this scenario, the court will appoint someone to manage the union on an interim basis until a full investigation is conducted by an impartial third person. However, there are serious risks. If it turns out that the concerns are unjustified, then the employee's future with both the union and the company is gone. It is not easy to take a matter to court, since invariably people will be upset and may well be alienated.

Unionized employees are governed by collective agreements that set out the terms and conditions of employment. In the event of a layoff or firing, severance is clearly spelled out. The collective agreement is very similar to a contract between the employer and the employee, and its purpose is to avoid any disputes between them. Nonetheless, there is a mechanism to deal with disputes.

Work Product

Q: An employee is being denied access to design work produced for the company and is wondering how she can obtain access to her work product (she did not keep copies of her designs).

A: If the work is done as a contractor or an employee, then the product belongs to the company, which can refuse to provide copies since it owns the product. There may be issues of copyright and protection of the product. Short of keeping copies of all work or ensuring that the terms of employment allow for access, there is little that she can do. However, if she leaves the place of work and is able to re-create the designs from memory, without using any of the company's products, then she is fully entitled to do so. For example, employees cannot take customer lists; however, they can re-create a good part of a list by using a readily available telephone book, since they are re-creating it using an outside source and their own abilities.

Extra Work

Q: A municipal employee is required, as part of her job, to attend council meetings. At one meeting, she is advised that her employment will be terminated and is presented with a letter, which includes a severance package and a release. The municipality is outside the main metropolitan areas, and the employee is over 55 years of age. What are the implications of this termination?

A: First, the courts have said that an employer must let an employee go in a fair and reasonable manner. In terminating the employee in a public forum, her reputation will be affected, and word will spread quickly that she no longer works for the municipality. Second, given her age and the small community, the prospects of reemployment are reduced. In determining a severance package, one looks firstly at the years of service and second at the surrounding circumstances. In this case, she will be entitled to one month for each year of service plus a few months given the manner of termination and the reduced prospects of reemployment.

Q: An employee working for a company received regular wages. The company asked her to train for a higher-paying job within the company. She performed the regular duties of her job and trained for another one. There were no overtime rules within the company, and the question is whether the employer can force the employee to work two jobs while receiving the salary for one.

A: If there is a contract or collective agreement, it will cover the rules and regulations for employee training. If it is silent on this issue, or if there is no written agreement, the employer is not required to pay a higher wage during training, is not required to pay overtime if it is not usually paid, and is not required to pay the higher wage until the employee is actually promoted. The best scenario is to discuss the situation with the boss and sort it out before bad feelings begin to fester.

Work Environment

Q: An employee works in a small basement with six other employees. One of the workers has persistent body odour. Some of the workers have spoken about this employee to company management, but the situation has not been rectified. Obviously, the other employees can quit, but they will then be unemployed. What can be done?

A: The law requires employers to provide a safe work environment. This is clearly not a safe environment as there is a persistent odour in the air. One alternative is to contact the Ministry of Labour to inspect the job site to determine whether or not it is safe. Alternatively, the employees can band together and bring an action in court to have the situation remedied.

Q: A prison guard is told that he has chronic lung disease, which in most cases is caused by smoking. He does not smoke but works in a small jail where the inmates constantly smoke. There is poor ventilation, and the treating physicians believe that the lung disease has been caused by second-hand smoke. The provincial government has a policy that guarantees employees a smoke-free workplace, but it is not enforcing this guarantee. What can the employee do?

A: Employers must provide a safe and healthy work environment. Governments can have different standards if they are reasonable. The government in this case is not enforcing a common standard. The employee can sue on his behalf and on behalf of all other prison guards who are faced with the same work environment, which clearly affects their health. Recently, however, in another province, when the government attempted to enforce the no-smoking policy, the prisoners rioted, causing millions of dollars in damage. The issue is still unresolved.

Qualifications

Q: What is the effect of an employer's misstating an employee's qualifications in a letter of reference?

A: Employers must be honest in giving a reference. If they overstate an employee's qualifications, and the employee fails in the new job, then the new employer can sue the old employer for misrepresentation. If they understate the qualifications, either out of spite or in an effort to get the employee back, then the employee can sue the old employer for interference with his or her right to work. For example, if in the old job an employee injured her back, and the new job requires lifting, then the old employer should disclose this fact. If a medical condition exists that is unrelated to the new job, then the employer can remain silent due to employee confidence unless directly asked the question. The bottom line is that employers should be both careful and honest.

Q: What personal information on an employee can be shared between employers?

A: Although there are rules governing privacy of personal information, it often becomes a matter of degree and depends on each case. If the information in the file affects an employee's new job, then the old employer risks being sued if he or she does not disclose this information to the new company. If it is unrelated, then an employee can insist that it remain confidential. It is often a fine line, and if in doubt an employer may disclose information in order to avoid being sued down the road.

Here is a sample letter of a positive reference.

Dear Sir/Madam:

Simon has worked for Acme Bird Seed Company for the past three years. During that time, he has been prompt and courteous and has carried out his assigned tasks.

Due to a corporate reorganization, we were unable to offer Simon continued employment. We would, however, recommend him to any prospective employer.

If there are any questions concerning his work experience, please do not hesitate to give us a call.

Here is a sample letter of reference that is not so positive. Further inquiries would be warranted.

Dear Sir/Madam:

Simon has worked for Acme Bird Seed Company for the past three years.

Acme Bird Seed Company grows, harvests, packages, and sells bird seed for all manner of birds, including road runners. Simon worked in the packaging department.

We would recommend Simon to other employers.

Conclusion

I hope that with this series of books, we have met the objective of providing basic information on questions that we all face when we come up against legal problems and issues. I hope that it will save you time and money when you need to consult a lawyer.

I also hope that you won't need to hire a lawyer, as it often means that you have a problem. Most matters can be resolved on your own by a letter or phone call. If not, then you *should* consult a lawyer, if only to clarify your rights. Then consider your options, as legal proceedings can be time consuming, emotionally draining, and costly.

For further information, your local courthouse will have pamphlets on basic rights, and the court staff is there to help you. Most government agencies are listed in the blue pages of your phone book. Courts and provincial law societies can be accessed on the World Wide Web. Use your favourite search engine and search for "court" or "law society" in your province. The Supreme Court of Canada has a web page located at www.scc-csc.gc.ca. Your local library will also have basic legal texts covering most areas of the law.

Thank you for using this book as a resource.

I hope that I have answered many of your legal questions. However, if your particular question needs to be answered or if there are follow-up issues that need to be addressed, you can write to me via the Internet by logging on to www.legalcounsel.ca.

Index